VISUAL QUICKSTART GUIDE

PageMaker 6

FOR WINDOWS

David Browne

Peachpit Press

PageMaker 6 for Windows
Visual QuickStart Guide
David Browne

Peachpit Press
2414 Sixth Street
Berkeley, CA 94710
510/548-4393
510/548-5991 (fax)

Find us on the World Wide Web at:
http://www.peachpit.com

Peachpit Press is a division of
Addison-Wesley Publishing Company.

Copyright © 1996 by David Browne

Cover design: The Visual Group

Notice of Rights

Notice of Liability

ISBN 0-201-88427-5

9 8 7 6 5 4 3 2 1

 Printed on recycled paper

Printed and bound in the United States of America

Dedication

To Sally, Michael and Kathleen

Acknowledgments

I would be remiss if I did not thank all the folks at Peachpit who helped with this book, especially Roslyn Bullas and Ted Nace.

Thanks once again to my wife Sally, who keeps me honest.

Table of Contents

Table of Contents

Table of Contents

Table of Contents

Getting Started

I LOVE THIS PROGRAM for its versatility. PageMaker 6.0 is lightning fast to start a fresh page, add text, and pile on graphics. It's easy to glide through specifying type and formatting paragraphs. Setting up for printing is logical and well thought out, and PageMaker prints gracefully, without fuss or bother. Yet, for all its ease in handling complex jobs, it is tempting to use PageMaker as a straight word processor—and it comes with enough templates to make business letters, envelopes and labels a breeze.

PageMaker is as adept at designing your resume as it is creating a complex, four-color magazine ad (or the magazine itself, for that matter). It can handle practically any creative design challenge you give it, yet crank out technical manuals and complete books—as it has with this *Visual QuickStart Guide*—camera-ready for printing and binding. PageMaker has a clean, straightforward layout window that's easy to learn and quick to use. The brilliance of PageMaker's design is that its powerful features don't clutter and confuse. Regardless of how little you know now, PageMaker will ease you gently into the sometimes turbulent waters of document publishing.

- There's nothing tricky or complicated that takes long hours of practice to learn in PageMaker.

- PageMaker's floating palettes make it easy to customize the look of the document window, with just the tools you want.

- Plug-ins let you add specialized commands, and update PageMaker's functionality (you can even add Photoshop plug-ins).

- PageMaker's Control palette helps you be as accurate and precise as you need to be (it's also a great way to format type on the fly).

Plus, PageMaker 6.0 includes tools to group and ungroup objects, align objects systematically, standardize colors between your computer's monitor and the printed page, even control trapping with a new trapping dialog box. So turn on your computer and let's get started...

Starting PageMaker

1 Click the Windows Start button to open the Start menu **(Figure 1)**.

2 Choose the Programs folder to open the Programs menu. Click on the Adobe folder to open its menu **(Figure 2)**.

3 Choose the PageMaker program icon. In a moment you will see the PageMaker title appear, and the program will open the layout window **(Figure 3)**.

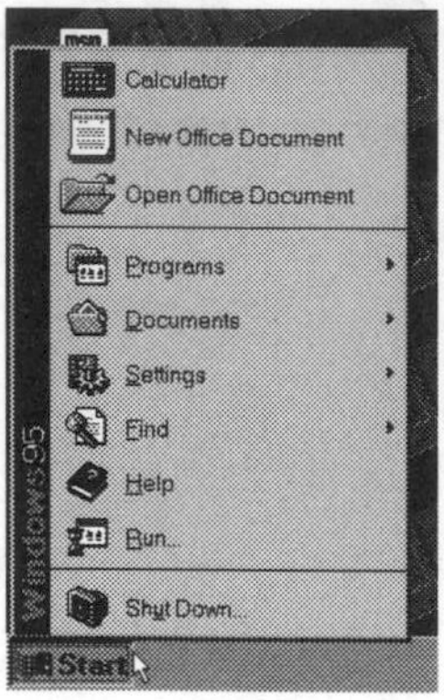

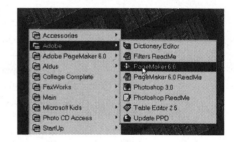

Figure 1 *Click the Windows 95 Start button to open the Start menu.*

Figure 2 *Opened PageMaker folder showing PageMaker program icon and other program icons.*

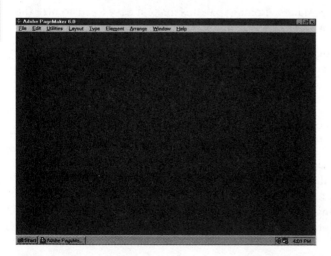

Figure 3 *PageMaker initially displays its menu bar and a blank layout window, when first started.*

Starting PageMaker

The Document Layout Window

Once PageMaker starts, you will normally open an existing document, or create a new document (explained in Chapter 2). **Figure 4** shows the window and its parts.

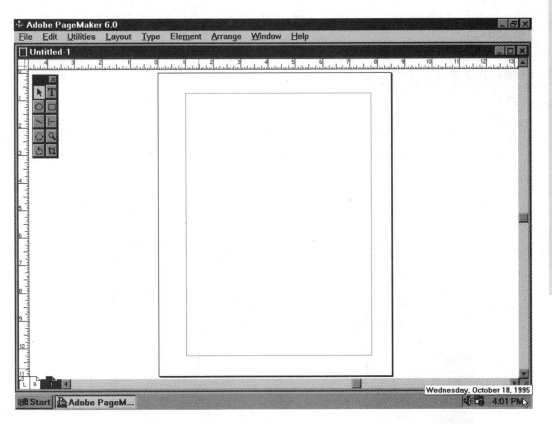

Figure 4 *PageMaker's document layout window.*

Using PageMaker's Menus

PageMaker's command menus are housed in the menu bar along the top of the application. Command menus are the source of all commands—click open a menu and, keeping the mouse button depressed, slide the mouse arrow down the menu to highlight the command you want. When the command is reversed in black, release the button to activate the command.

File Menu

You will find basic housekeeping chores here, with commands that open and save documents, set preferences and print your work **(Figure 5)**.

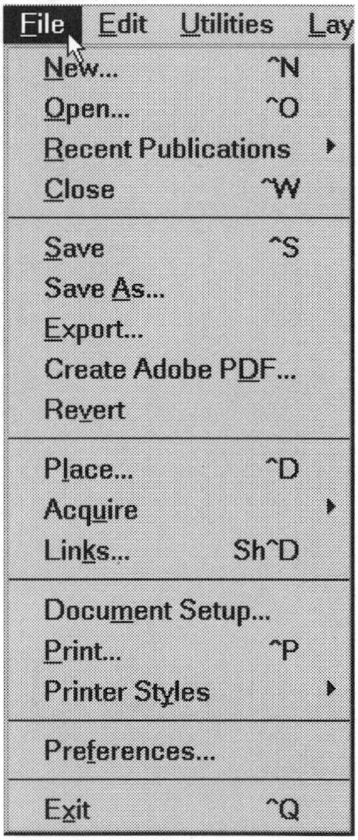

Edit Menu

Use these commands to help edit text, and paste text and objects onto your pages **(Figure 6)**. The Edit menu holds the Undo command, that can usually undo your last mistake, and the Select All command that selects every object on the page.

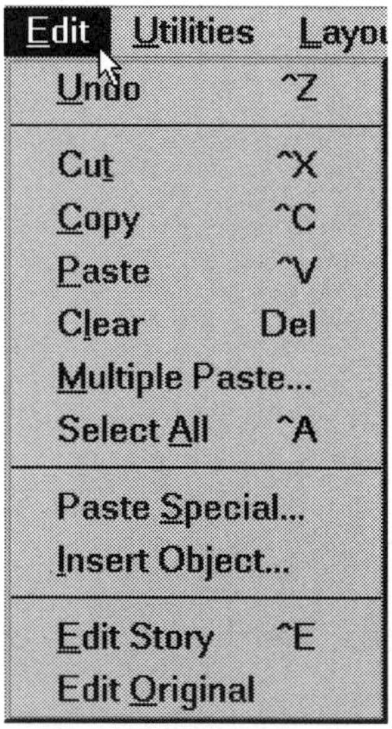

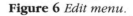

Figure 5 *File menu.*

Figure 6 *Edit menu.*

Using the Menus

Utilities Menu

This menu contains a number of Adobe Plug-ins—specialized programs that do specific tasks for you, such as creating running headers and footers, or drop caps. The menu also handles PageMaker's indexing and trapping tools **(Figure 7)**.

Layout Menu

Use the commands here to manage the layout and pagination of your documents. You can add and delete pages, change views, control guides and rulers, and rearrange the order of pages **(Figure 8)**.

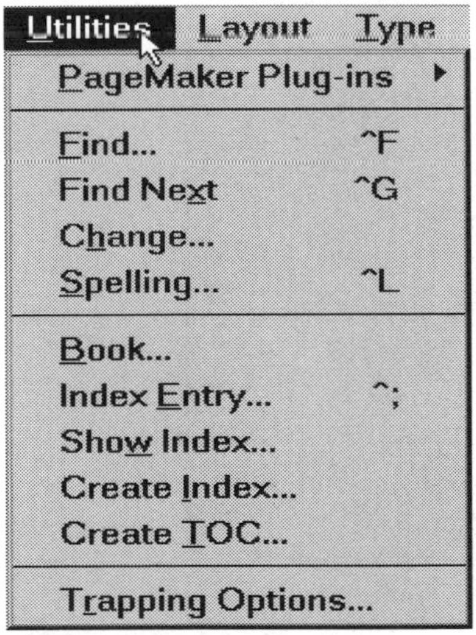

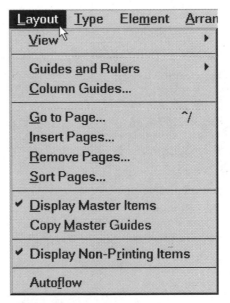

Figure 7 *Utilities menu.*

Figure 8 *Layout menu.*

Type Menu

All of PageMaker's powerful typographic tools are found on this menu. You will also set tabs here and control hyphenation. Finally, styles are selected and defined on the Type menu **(Figure 9)**.

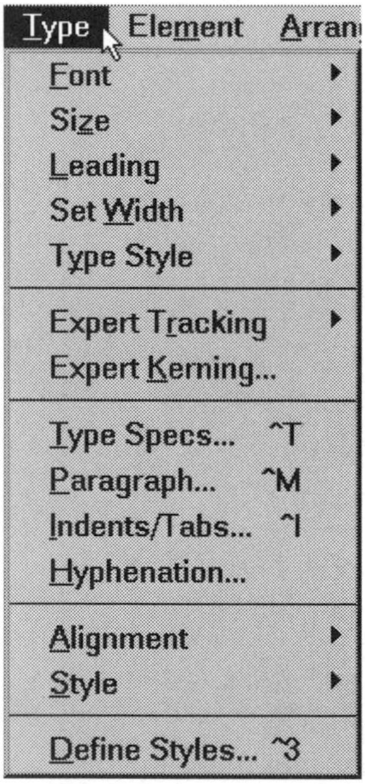

Element Menu

Think of this as basically the graphic menu. It handles color, lines and fills; it modifies images and controls masking **(Figure 10)**. Color is defined here, and you will control how text wraps around graphics with the Element menu.

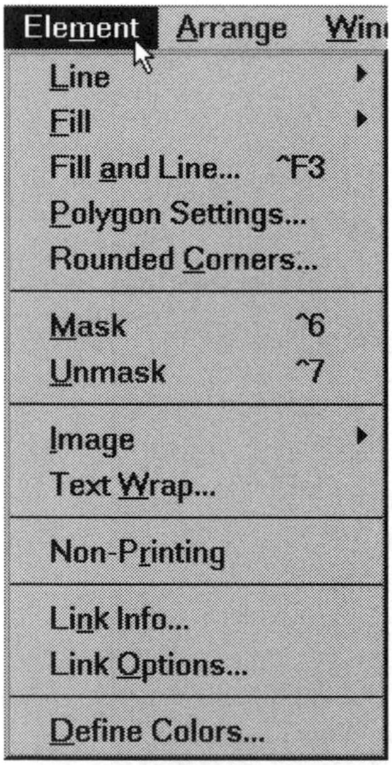

Using the Menus

Figure 9 *Type menu.*

Figure 10 *Element menu.*

Arrange Menu

The commands on this menu control how objects are layered on top of one another. You can combine objects into groups and objects can be positioned in relation to each other **(Figure 11)**.

Window Menu

Go to this menu whenever you want to open one of PageMaker's many floating palettes **(Figure 12)**. You choose which opened document you want to work on using the Window menu.

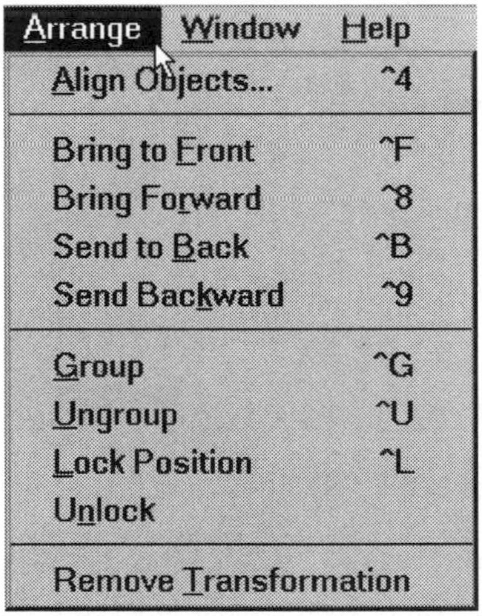

Figure 11 *Arrange menu.*

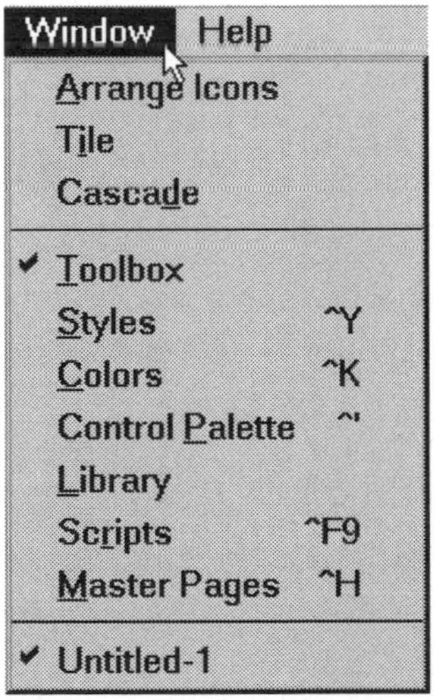

Figure 12 *Window menu.*

About PageMaker's Tools

PageMaker's toolbox **(Figure 13)** holds the common tools you will use to design and produce pages.

- **Pointer tool**—selects objects and moves or re-sizes them. Clicking text selects it, and displays the text block (explained in Chapter 3). Selected items display sizing handles **(Figure 14)**. Click a handle with the Pointer tool and drag the handle to re-size the object **(Figure 15)**.

- **Text tool**—creates new text and highlights existing text. When you choose the text tool the cursor changes to an I-beam text insertion point. Wherever you click the I-beam will be the starting point for typing new text. To highlight text, click and drag across the words you want **(Figure 16)**. To highlight single words, double-click. To highlight a paragraph, triple-click the paragraph.

- **Ellipse tool**—draws ellipses (ovals) and circles.

- **Rectangle tool**—draws rectangles and squares.

- **Line tool**—draws straight lines at any angle.

- **Constrained-line tool**—draws only horizontal or vertical lines.

- **Polygon tool**—creates polygons (closed shapes with three or more sides).

- **Zoom tool**—lets you see the page at different magnifications or reductions.

- **Rotating tool**—rotates text and graphics.

- **Cropping tool**—trims away unwanted parts of graphics, much like using an X-Acto knife.

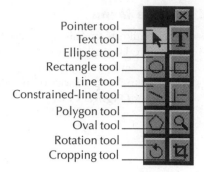

Pointer tool
Text tool
Ellipse tool
Rectangle tool
Line tool
Constrained-line tool
Polygon tool
Oval tool
Rotation tool
Cropping tool

Figure 13 *PageMaker's toolbox.*

Figure 14 *Selecting with the Pointer tool shows the objects sizing handles.*

Figure 15 *Drag a sizing handle to re-size the object.*

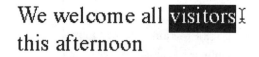

We welcome all visitors this afternoon

Figure 16 *Use the Text tool I-beam to highlight text.*

Using Tools

Using Dialog Boxes

Dialog boxes are your chief means of communicating with PageMaker. Dialog boxes will generally hold a number of possible choices; you pick and choose among the choices to define exactly what you want to do. A good example is the Type Specifications dialog box **(Figure 17),** which uses a number of list boxes, menus and check boxes to format type exactly the way you want it.

Check boxes offer options you can turn off and on by clicking

List boxes pop up or down to display a menu of choices

Dialog box buttons open additonal, related dialog boxes

OK button activates your choices and takes you back to your document

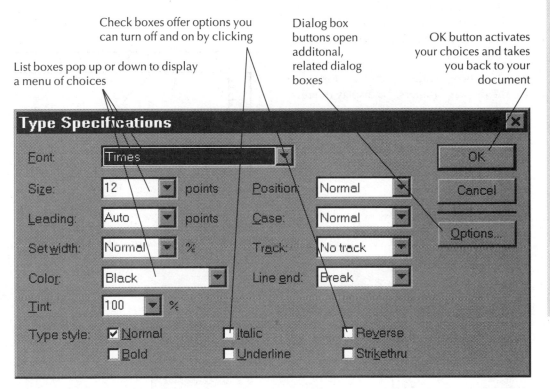

Figure 17 *Type Specifications dialog box uses a number of dialog box tools to format type.*

Using Rulers

By default, PageMaker displays a vertical and a horizontal ruler **(Figure 18)**. Rulers help you accurately align text and graphics on the page. Notice that, regardless of the tool selected, wherever you move the tool, position marks move on the rules an equal amount **(Figure 19)**. The tick marks show the relative vertical and horizontal positions of the tool as it moves around the page, or as you drag objects to specific positions. To display or hide the rulers:

1 Click open the Layout menu and choose the Guides and Rulers command **(Figure 20)**. You will see a submenu open **(Figure 21)**.

2 The **Show Rulers** command controls the display of rulers. To display the rulers, click to add a check. To hide rulers, click the checked command to remove the check mark.

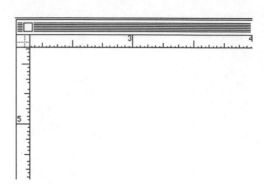

Figure 18 *PageMaker's horizontal and vertical rulers.*

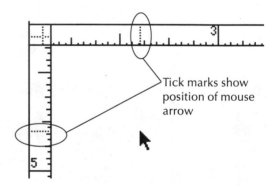

Tick marks show position of mouse arrow

Figure 19 *Tick marks on the rulers show the constant position of the mouse icon.*

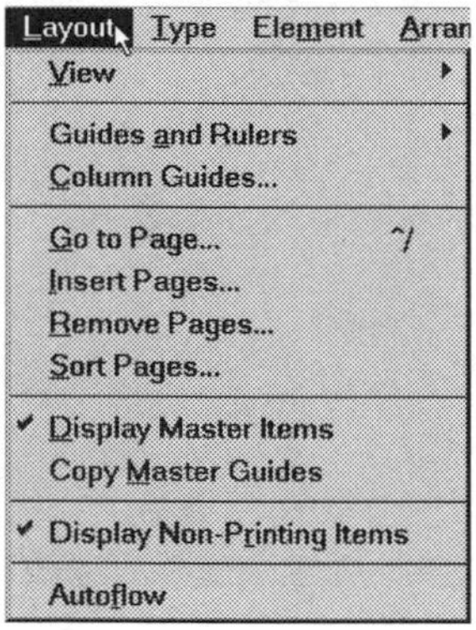

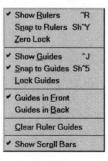

Figure 20 *Choose Guides and Rulers command on the Layout menu.*

Figure 21 *Guides and Rulers submenu.*

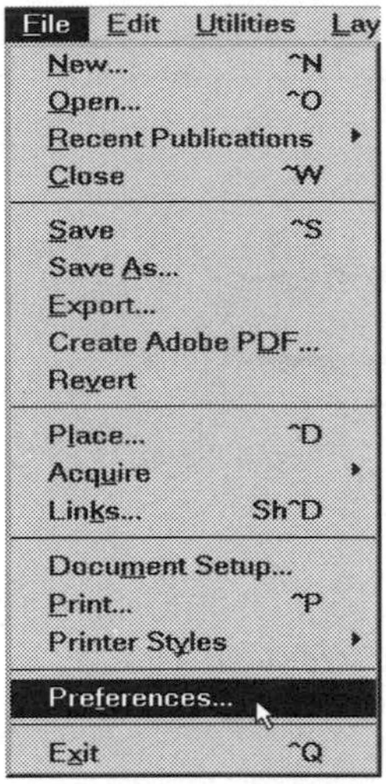

File	Edit	Utilities	Lay

New...   ^N
Open...   ^O
Recent Publications   ▶
Close   ^W

Save   ^S
Save As...
Export...
Create Adobe PDF...
Revert

Place...   ^D
Acquire   ▶
Links...   Sh^D

Document Setup...
Print...   ^P
Printer Styles   ▶

Preferences...

Exit   ^Q

Figure 22 *Choose the Preferences command on the File menu.*

Changing Ruler Measurement Systems

If inches seem awkward to use, you can choose among a number of measurement systems for the two rulers, including picas, millimeters, and decimal inches (10 marks to the inch instead of eight).

1 Click open the File menu and choose the Preferences command **(Figure 22)**. You will see the Preferences dialog box **(Figure 23)**.

2 The measurement systems are controlled by the Measurements in, and Vertical ruler boxes. To set the default measuring system throughout PageMaker—including the rulers, click the **Measurements in** box to open the list of measurements **(Figure 24)**. To have a different measuring system just for the vertical ruler, click open the **Vertical ruler** box **(Figure 25)** and make your choice.

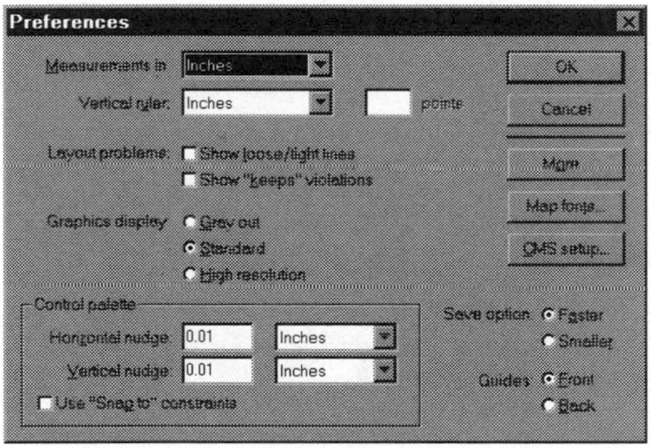

Preferences

Measurements in   Inches
Vertical ruler: Inches   points

Layout problems: ☐ Show loose/tight lines
                   ☐ Show "keeps" violations

Graphics display   ○ Grey out
                   ● Standard
                   ○ High resolution

Control palette
Horizontal nudge: 0.01   Inches
Vertical nudge: 0.01   Inches
☐ Use "Snap to" constraints

Save option ● Faster
             ○ Smaller
Guides ● Front
        ○ Back

OK
Cancel
More
Map fonts...
CMS setup...

Figure 23 *Use the Preferences dialog box to select the ruler measurement system.*

Inches decimal

Inches
Inches decimal
Millimeters
Picas
Ciceros

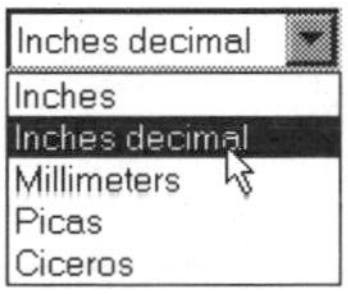

Figure 24
Horizontal ruler and dialog boxes are controlled by Measurement In list box.

Picas

Inches
Inches decimal
Millimeters
Picas
Ciceros
Custom

Figure 25
Change just the vertical ruler system with the Vertical ruler list box.

Using Rulers

Resetting the Ruler Zero Point

As I already mentioned, the default rulers measure the relative position of objects on the page—relative to the upper left corner of the page. But, by repositioning the zero-point intersection of the horizontal and vertical rulers, you can use the rulers to measure the size of objects, like boxes and lines, or position guidelines for precise positioning. To reset the zero point:

1 Move the mouse up and to the left to the intersecting corner of the two rulers, called the zero point **(Figure 26)**.

2 Click and drag the zero point across the page to align it with whatever you want to measure **(Figure 27)**.

3 As you drag the zero point, dotted horizontal and vertical lines, looking like a huge cross hair, will help to accurately position the new zero point **(Figure 28)**.

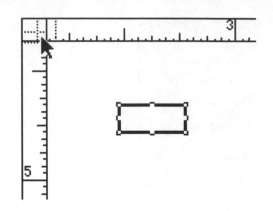

Figure 26 *Rulers' zero point is the intersection of horizontal and vertical rulers.*

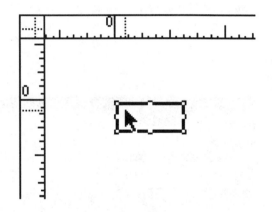
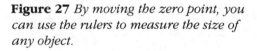

Figure 27 *By moving the zero point, you can use the rulers to measure the size of any object.*

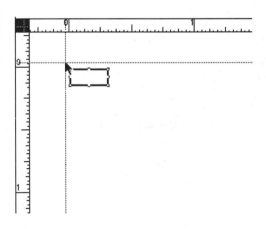

Figure 28 *Dragging the zero point displays dotted alignment guidelines that help you reset the rulers.*

Using Rulers

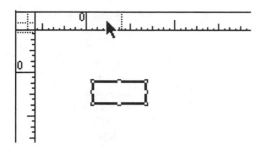

Figure 29 *Move the mouse pointer over either ruler to grab a new guide.*

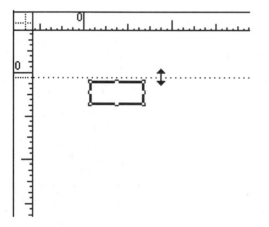

Figure 30 *Click and drag the guide anywhere on the page (tick marks on both rulers show the guides exact position).*

Using Guidelines

Guidelines (called *guides* in PageMaker) are non-printing blue lines you can use to help align text and graphics on your pages. The rulers store an unlimited number of guides. To find them, simply drag them out of the rulers. Here's how:

1 Move the mouse pointer to either the horizontal or vertical ruler (horizontal guides are found in the horizontal ruler; vertical guides are in the vertical ruler). Regardless of the tool selected, the mouse icon will change to an arrow once it's over a ruler **(Figure 29)**.

2 Click and hold down the mouse button. The arrow will change to a two-way vertical or horizontal arrow (depending on which ruler you are over).

3 Now drag the two-way arrow down, out of the horizontal ruler, or to the right, out of the vertical ruler. You will see a dotted guide line attached to the arrow **(Figure 30)**.

4 Drag the guide to wherever you need it. Notice the tick mark on the opposite ruler that the guide came out of. The tick mark shows you the exact measurement on the ruler for accurate alignments.

Tips

◼ If you have trouble resetting the zero point of the rulers, try positioning a horizontal and a vertical guide first, then adjust the cross hair of the ruler zero point over the guides.

◼ If the guides are in your way, use the Pointer tool to drag them back to their respective rulers, out of the way. A quick shortcut to turn the display of guides off and on is **Ctrl+J**.

Using Guides

Snapping Objects to Rulers and Guides

PageMaker has a magnetic force field built into rulers and guides. Called the snap-to feature, it draws objects like a magnet snapping up paper clips. When snap-to is activated, all you have to do is move an object close to a ruler or guide, and the magnetic pull will literally snap it to the closest ruler tick mark or guide. Here's how to activate the snap-to feature:

1   Click open the Layout menu and choose the Guides and Rulers command **(Figure 31)**.

2   PageMaker will open the Guides and Rulers submenu **(Figure 32)**.

3   A check mark next to the Snap to Rulers, or Snap to Guides command indicates the feature is active. Choose either command again to remove the check mark and turn the feature off.

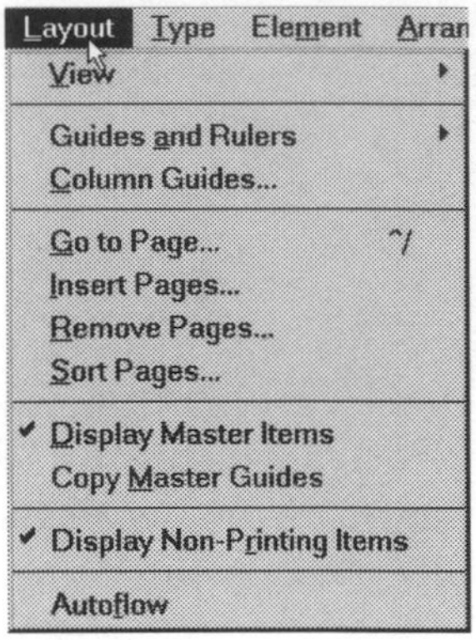

Tip

■ Use the snap-to feature to snap rulers to guides and guides to rulers. For instance, when resetting the ruler zero point, first drag out some guides to align the zero point cross hair to and turn on snap-to. When the cross hair gets close to the guides they will snap to the guides automatically. Likewise, with snap-to on, the guides you drag will snap to the exact ruler tick marks you want.

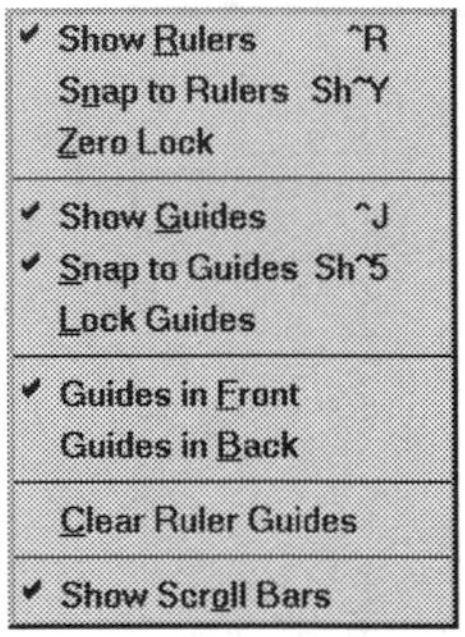

Figure 31 *Choose the Guides and Rulers command on the Layout menu.*

Figure 32 *Guides and Rulers submenu.*

Using Guides

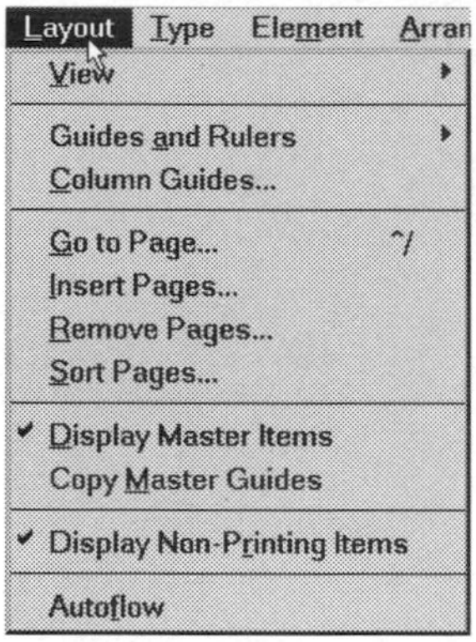

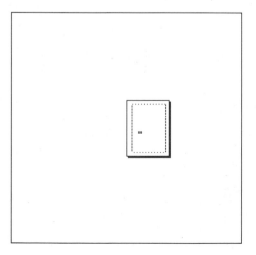

Figure 33 *Choose the View command on the Layout menu.*

About the Pasteboard

The pasteboard is PageMaker's analogy to working on a drawing board. You can see the entire pasteboard by opening the Layout menu and choosing the View command **(Figure 33)**. In the View submenu, choose Entire Pasteboard. You will see the 46-by-46 inch pasteboard with the document page in the center **(Figure 34)**.

Tips

▰ The pasteboard is a great temporary storage area for text and graphics. When you save your document, PageMaker also saves anything remaining on the pasteboard, so objects can be left there permanently without worry that they will be lost.

▰ Write reminders to yourself on the pasteboard as the design and production of your document develops.

▰ Use the pasteboard to store special bullets, dingbats or doodads.

▰ Store recurring text on the pasteboard. Then it's easy to click and copy the text back to the Clipboard.

Figure 34 *Document centered on PageMaker's pasteboard (Entire Pasteboard view).*

Using the Pasteboard

Quick and Easy Work Habits

■ The quickest way to use guides is generally to reset the ruler zero point first. Then drag out as many guides as you need for alignment. Finally, click and drag the object you are aligning over to the guides to position it accurately.

■ To turn the snap-to rulers and snap-to guides commands off and on, use these shortcuts:

Snap-to Rulers **Ctrl+Shift+Y**
Snap-to Guides **Ctrl+Shift+5**

■ You may find PageMaker's snap to feature to be a nuisance when you are making very fine alignments. Just turn it off momentarily, finish adjusting the object, and then turn snap-to back on.

■ You may also find it helpful to go to a higher view magnification for extremely close alignments. Try 400% (choose View on the Layout menu to see the View submenu). To double the view to 800%, click the **Zoom tool** in the toolbox. The mouse icon will change to a magnifying glass. Then, click and drag an outline around the object to magnify and release.

■ To change the global default settings in PageMaker, make the changes when PageMaker is started, but before a document is created or opened. Changes to settings made while a document is open affect only that document.

■ Shortcuts to remember:

Create New Document **Ctrl+N**
Save Document **Ctrl+S**
Display Guides On/Off **Ctrl+J**
Display Rulers On/Off **Ctrl+R**
Fit in Window View Size **Ctrl+0**
50% View Size **Ctrl+5**
Actual View Size **Ctrl+1**
200% View Size **Ctrl+2**

Quick Work Tips

Starting a Document

PAGEMAKER MAKES IT EXTREMELY easy to create a new document: Define some basic things in only one dialog box and PageMaker creates a new, blank document page, or as many pages as you think you'll need. More pages can be easily added or deleted as your design progresses, while multiple master pages control common text or graphics. And, you can change page sizes, margin settings, even page number parameters at any time to accommodate your needs.

This chapter helps you define the page, gets you up and running with a new document, and covers the essentials of controlling text and graphics. You'll learn about setting up master pages to control recurring elements, how to set margins, even how to decide the overall size of your new document. And, once a single page is defined, it's a simple matter to add as many more pages as you require.

Introduction

Creating a New Document

Configuring new documents in PageMaker is easy and straightforward:

1 Click the File menu to open it **(Figure 1)**. Move the mouse arrow over the New command and click to choose the command.

2 PageMaker will display the Document Setup dialog box **(Figure 2)**. Notice the default settings in the dialog box configure an 8½-by-11 inch page. To change the default setup for your new document:

▪ **Dimensions**—You can change the overall page size by entering a different width and height in the two text boxes. Click open the Page size list box to see a list of pre-configured page sizes.

▪ **Page Orientation**—To lay out your document with the page turned (so the longer sides are the top and bottom), click the Wide radio button.

▪ **Margins**—Change the default margin settings to what you want. Note that inside and outside margins become left and right margins if you disable the Double-sided option (click to remove the check mark).

▪ **Number of pages**—PageMaker automatically starts with one page; add as many as you want now, or you can add them later.

3 Click OK to save your changes and create the new document.

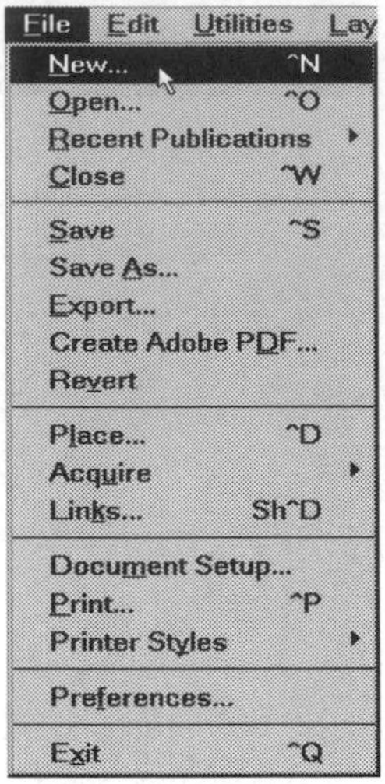

Figure 1 *Choose New command on the File menu.*

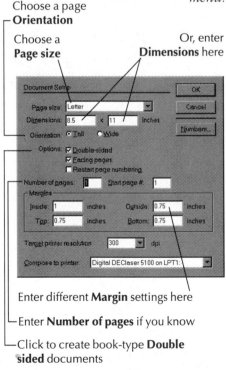

Choose a page
Orientation

Choose a
Page size

Or, enter
Dimensions here

Enter different **Margin** settings here

Enter **Number of pages** if you know

Click to create book-type **Double sided** documents

Figure 2 *Document Setup dialog box.*

Creating a New Document

About Page Sizes

There are really two page sizes to think about in PageMaker: the size of the document page in PageMaker's document window and the physical size of the paper running through your laser printer. Often the sizes are the same, but they may differ, depending on the type of document you want to design. The table below shows some examples of documents requiring different sizes for the design, versus the printed results.

- Designed Page Size—Choose the size of the actual page you will design in the Document Setup dialog box.

- Printed Page Size—Choose the overall size of the paper being printed by your printer in the Print dialog box

Choosing a Page Size

Document Type	Designed Page Size	Printed Page Size	Folded?	Trimmed?
Book	7 by 9	8 ½ by 11	no	yes
Flyer	5 ½ by 8 ½	11 by 8 ½	yes	no
Business card	2 by 3 ½	8 ½ by 11 (Printed 8 up on page)	no	yes
Invitation	4 by 5	8 ½ by 11 (Printed 4 up on page)	no	yes

Setting Margins

Margins generally define a border between text and the edges of the page. Margins are measured from the edge of the page inward. You can change margins at anytime, but doing so may cause text to shift on the page unexpectedly.

1 Choose the File menu and click the Document Setup command **(Figure 3)**.

2 In the Document Setup dialog box **(Figure 4)**, enter new values in the margin text boxes.

3 You can enter values in any measurement system recognized by PageMaker (the table below shows how to indicate the system you want).

Tip

◼ PageMaker will convert the measurement value you enter in the text box to the default system specified in the Preferences dialog box. To see the converted margin values, choose Document Setup on the File menu and notice the margin values. The values you entered in a different system are converted automatically.

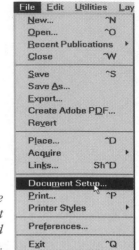

Figure 3 *Choose the Document Setup command on the File menu.*

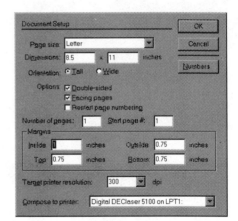

Figure 4 *Add the margin measurements you want in the Document Setup dialog box.*

Current system	Add this	To get this
Inches	i after the value	1i *for 1 inch*
Picas	p after value	6p *for 6 picas*
Points	p before value	p72 *for 72 points*
Picas and points	p between the values	12p3 *for 12 picas and 3 points*
Millimeters	m after the value	12m *for 12 millimeters*

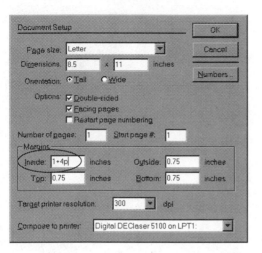

Figure 5 *Entering a formula in the Left margin text box, in the Document Setup dialog box (PageMaker will calculate the value when you click OK).*

Letting PageMaker Calculate Measurements

How to do a little math with measurements: PageMaker will add, subtract, multiply or divide measurement values for you. Simply enter the appropriate formula in the text box. For example, let's say you want the left margin a little wider. To increase the width by 4 picas, enter the formula **+4p** after the current left margin value in the Document Setup dialog box **(Figure 5)**. When you click OK, PageMaker will calculate the new value and move the left margin accordingly.

Type of calculation	Use this symbol	Like this
Addition	+	18p+6p3
Subtraction	-	18p-6p3
Multiplication	*	18p*1.2
Division	/	18p/2

Calculating Measurements

Adding More Pages

When you start a new document in the Document Setup dialog box, PageMaker automatically creates a one-page document. You can enter the total number of pages if you know, or start out with just one page and add more as you need them. Here's how:

1 Select the Layout menu **(Figure 6)** and choose the Insert Pages command to open the Insert Pages dialog box **(Figure 7)**.

2 Enter the number of pages you want to add in the **Insert** text box.

3 Then, choose whether you want the pages added before or after the current page, by selecting the choice in the list box.

4 To assign a master page to the newly added pages, choose it from the Master page list box.

5 Click **Insert** to add the page(s).

Tip

▪ Since PageMaker inserts pages relative to the page you are working on, always first move to the page of your document you want to add pages before, after or between (if your document is configured with double-sided pages).

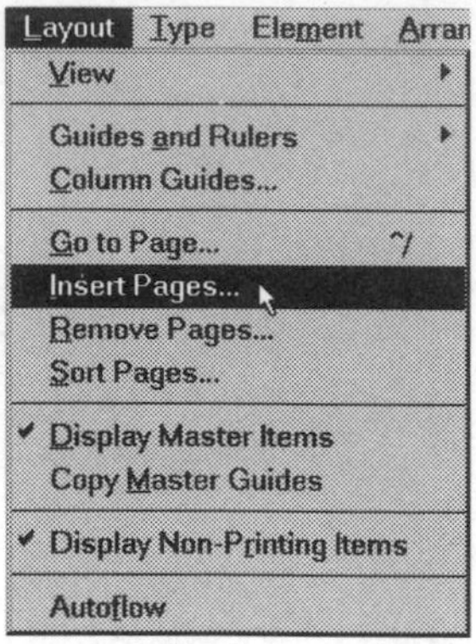

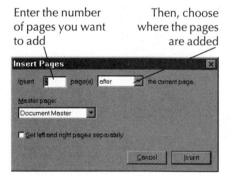

Figure 6 *Choose Insert Pages command on the Layout menu.*

Enter the number of pages you want to add

Then, choose where the pages are added

Figure 7 *Add pages to your document with the Insert Pages dialog box.*

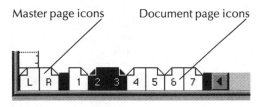

Master page icons   Document page icons

Figure 8 *Click the master page icons to move to your document's master pages.*

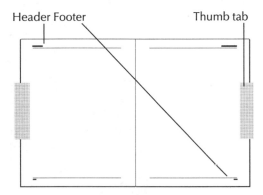

Header Footer   Thumb tab

Figure 9 *Master pages for this book.*

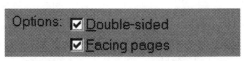

Figure 10 *Options area in Document Setup dialog box.*

Setting Up Master Pages

A master page holds common items found on more than one page. For instance, if guidelines that indicate text alignment will be needed for most, if not all of your pages, add them to a master page. If text recurs on most pages, such as with headers or footers, add the text to a master page. If a logo or special graphic is needed in the same place on more than one page, put the graphic on a master page. To create a master page:

1 Look at the bottom of the document layout window and click the master page icon, to the left of the document page icons **(Figure 8)**. Initially, the master page looks like any other blank document page in PageMaker. However, anything you add will appear on any or all of your document pages, depending on what you want.

2 Add the items you want to your master page. Your finished master page might look like the master page for this book, which includes several rules, the shaded thumb tabs, alternating headers, and the page number footer **(Figure 9)**.

Tip

■ The master page icon will have two pages if you have selected the facing pages option in the Document Setup dialog box **(Figure 10)**. If you have not checked the Facing pages check box, the master page icon will be a single page **(Figure 11)**.

Figure 11 *A single-sided document will only have one master page icon.*

Master Pages

Seeing Master Page Items on Document Pages

If you don't see the master page items when you move back to your document, it's because you haven't told PageMaker to display them. Here's how:

1 Choose the Layout menu **(Figure 12)**. The command Display Master Items is the culprit. With a check mark, items on the master pages would be shown.

2 Click the menu command to toggle it on and add the check mark **(Figure 13)**.

Tip

▪ The Display Master Items command on the layout menu affects only printable master page items, like text and graphics. Non-printing master page items are displayed by using the Copy Master Guides command on the same menu.

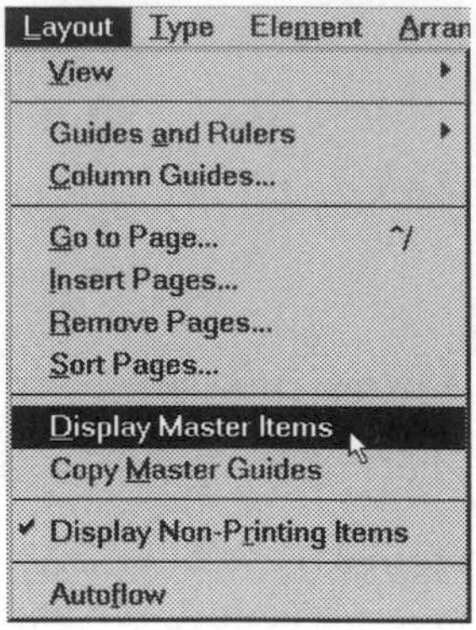

Figure 12 *To see master page items on document pages, choose Display Master Items command on Layout menu.*

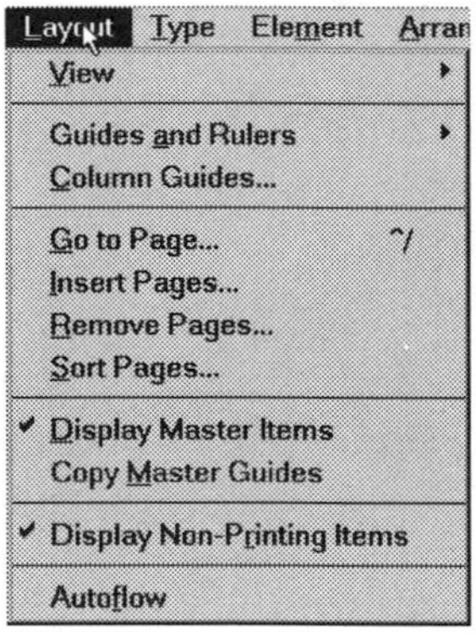

Figure 13 *Check mark beside Display Master Items command shows the feature is active.*

Master Pages

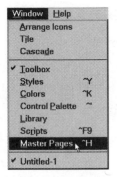

Figure 14 *Choose the Master Pages command on the Window menu.*

Figure 15 *Master Pages palette.*

Adding More Master Pages

While one master page is sufficient for many kinds of documents, sometimes having multiple master pages is the perfect solution to your design. For instance, a magazine could use one master page for all text pages holding editorial content, and a second master page for classified advertising. A truly wonderful improvement to PageMaker 6.0 is the ability to create as many different master pages as you need.

All additional master pages are controlled by the Master Pages palette. To open the palette:

1 Click open the Window menu **(Figure 14)** and choose the Master Pages command. In a moment you will see the palette **(Figure 15)**.

2 PageMaker lets you create additional master pages in two different ways:

■ By using an existing master page as the basis for a new master page

■ By opening a new, blank master page and adding items to it.

Tip

■ As you work, you may find that the Master Pages palette gets in your way and clutters up the document page. If so, drag it down to the bottom of the page and tuck all but the title bar under the edge of the document window **(Figure 16)**. Now it's out of your hair, but readily available.

Master Pages

Figure 16 *Master Pages palette tucked out of the way, but instantly available.*

Master Pages

Duplicating Additional Master Pages

If some items remain constant among your document pages, such as headers and footers, or graphics such as logos or lines, then it's easier to duplicate a new master page from an existing master page. Here's how:

1 Click the right-facing arrow in the Master Pages palette to open the menu **(Figure 17)**.

2 Choose the Duplicate command to open the Duplicate Master Page dialog box **(Figure 18)**.

3 Click open the Duplicate list box and choose the existing master page you want to copy.

4 Enter a new name for the master page in the Name of new master text box.

5 Choose **Duplicate** to copy the master page. The new master page will be added to the list in the palette.

6 Now, click the new name. Then, click the master page icon to open the new master page. Make the needed changes to the master pages you just duplicated, and you're done.

Tip

▪ When you have created more than one master page, the master page icon opens whichever master page you have selected in the Master Pages palette.

New Master...
Setup...
Duplicate...
Delete...

Apply...
Save Page as...

Prompt on Apply

Figure 17 *Master Pages menu.*

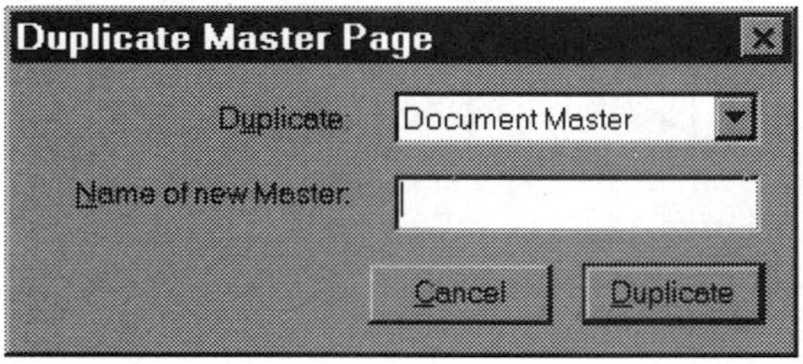

Figure 18 *Duplicate Master Page dialog box.*

New Master...
Setup...
Duplicate...
Delete...

Apply...
Save Page as...

Prompt on Apply

Figure 19 *Master Pages menu.*

Creating Additional Master Pages from Scratch

1 Click the right-facing arrow in the Master Pages palette **(Figure 19)** and choose the New master command. You will see the Create New Master Page dialog box **(Figure 20)**.

2 Name the master page, and make any changes you want to the margins, columns or space between the columns (*gutters*).

3 Click OK to create the master page. Then click the master page icon at the bottom of the document window to open the master page and add the items you want.

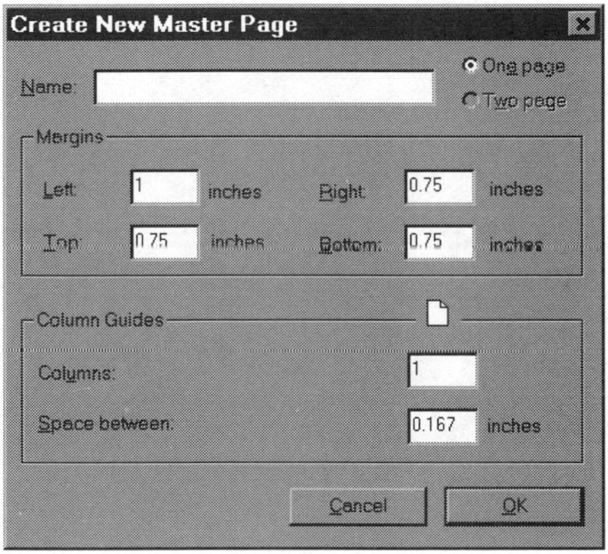

Master Pages

Create New Master Page

| Name: | ☐ | ⦿ One page |
| | | ○ Two page |

Margins

| Left: | 1 | inches | Right: | 0.75 | inches |
| Top: | 0.75 | inches | Bottom: | 0.75 | inches |

Column Guides

| Columns: | 1 |
| Space between: | 0.167 | inches |

Cancel   OK

Figure 20 *Create New Master Page dialog box.*

Handling Page Numbers

Page numbers are the most common item to be added to master pages. Why? Because, generally speaking, every page of a document should be numbered.

PageMaker will sequentially number your document pages if you add a code to the master page. And, it's infinitely easier to add PageMaker's page number code once to a master page than to manually number each page of a document. Here's how:

1 Click the master page icon to display the master page for your document.

2 Open the Layout menu and choose the 200% view from the View submenu.

3 Choose the Text tool and click where you want to add the page number.

4 Then, press the key combination **Ctrl+Shift+3** to add the page numbers. If you have set up your document with facing pages, you must add the page number code to both the left and right master page. Instead of a page number, you will see the code RM **(Figure 21)** or LM and RM on facing pages. Move back to your document to see the actual page numbers. *(Continued on next page.)*

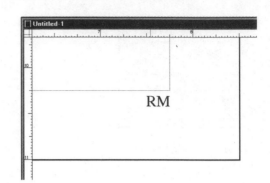

Figure 21 *Automatic page number code on master page indicates where real page numbers will be added on document pages.*

Page Numbers

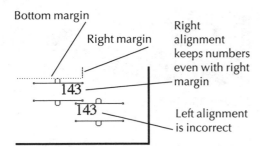

Bottom margin

Right margin

Right alignment keeps numbers even with right margin

Left alignment is incorrect

Figure 22 *Remember to align page numbers correctly (left-hand page numbers left-aligned, right-hand page numbers right-aligned).*

Tips

■ It does no good to simply type the two letters that the page number code creates on your master pages—you must press **Ctrl+Shift+3** to create automatic page numbers.

■ Any formatting you apply to the page number code on the master page formats the actual page numbers on your document pages. For example, if you highlight the marker and change it to bold italic, the actual page numbers will be bold and italic.

■ Whenever you position a page number code on the right side of the master page, remember to change its alignment to aligned-right so two-digit and three-digit page numbers will remain aligned with the right edge of the page and extend to the left **(Figure 22)**. To change alignment, open the Type menu and choose the **Alignment** command.

■ You can control the numbering system for document pages (Arabic, Roman Numeral, etc.) with the Document Setup dialog box. See Chapter 5 for details.

Page Numbers

Adding Headers and Footers

Any recurring text or graphics at the top or bottom of the page is considered a header or footer respectively. To create a header or footer:

1 Click the master page icon to open the master page **(Figure 23)**.

2 Magnify the view and move to the area of the page where the header or footer will be added **(Figure 24)**.

3 Add guides to help align the text or graphics in the header or footer **(Figure 25)**.

4 Type the text for the header or footer **(Figure 26)**.

Tips

■ You can edit or delete text in headers and footers at any time. Simply open the master page and make whatever changes you want. When you move back to your document pages, the changes will be reflected in the displayed headers and/or footers.

■ To set up alternating headers or footers (headers on odd pages are different from the headers on even pages), don't set up two different master pages. Instead, configure your document for facing pages (in the Document Setup dialog box), open the master page and put one header on the left-hand page and the alternative header on the right-hand page.

Figure 23 *Click the Master Page icon to open the Master Page.*

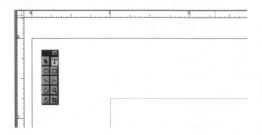

Figure 24 *Upper left corner of the Master Page, magnified, and ready to add a header.*

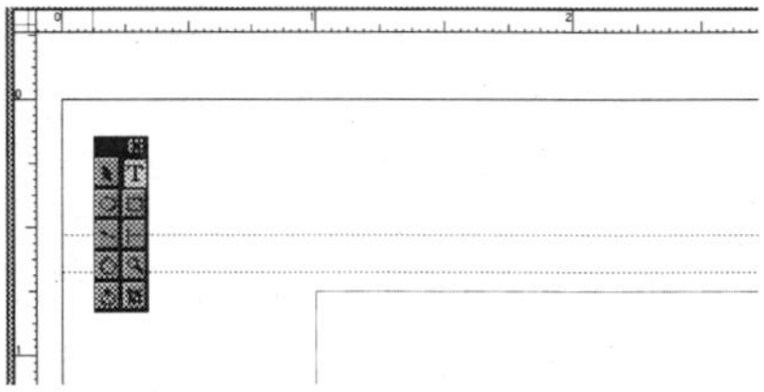

Figure 25 *Upper left corner of Master Page with guides added to help align the header.*

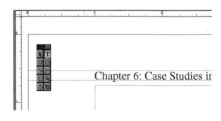

Figure 26 *Upper left corner of Master Page with header text added.*

Headers and Footers

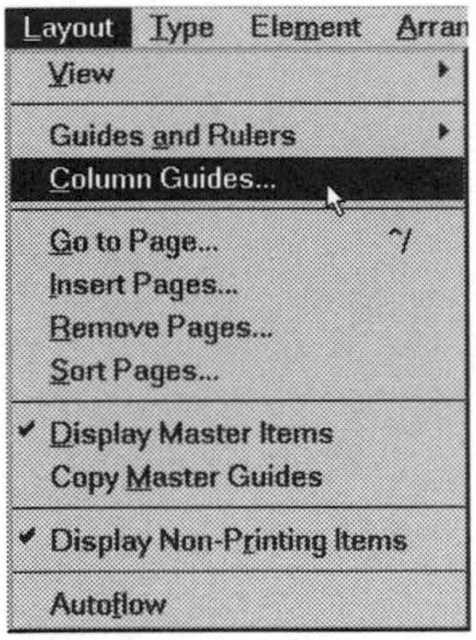

Adding Multiple Columns

PageMaker defines columns by the number of *column guides* you define on the page (think of column guides like vertical margins that define the width of each column). The default setup is one guide, or one column for text. Here's how to add more:

1 Move to the page you want to add columns to.

2 Select the Layout menu **(Figure 27)** and choose the Column Guides command.

3 PageMaker will open the Column Guides dialog box **(Figure 28)**. Enter the number of columns and amount of space between columns (known as the *gutter*).

4 Click OK to add the columns and return to your document.

Tips

▦ Since PageMaker deals with column definition on a page-by-page basis, the easy way to give all document pages multiple columns is to open the master page for your document, define the multiple columns, and insert the total number of pages you'll need for your document. All the pages you insert will carry the number of columns defined on your master page.

▦ To create unequal width columns, such as a narrow column for headings and a wide column for text relating to those headings, open the Column Guides dialog box and choose two columns. Then click and drag the column guide to widen one of the columns **(Figure 29)**. Do this on a master page to create the same unequal width columns for all your document pages.

Figure 27 *Choose the Column Guides command on the Layout menu.*

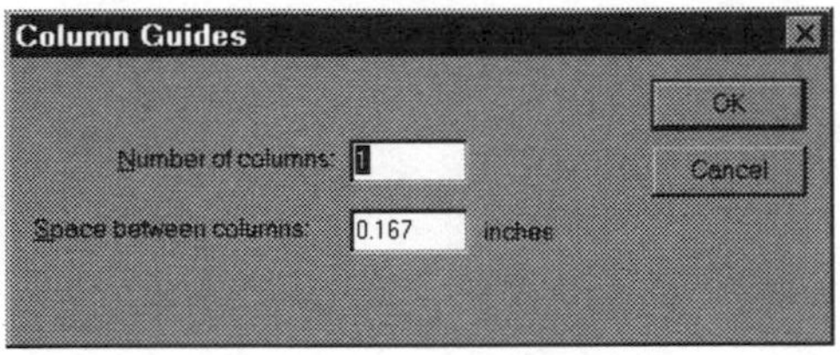

Figure 28 *Enter the number of columns in the Column Guides dialog box.*

Click and drag the column guide

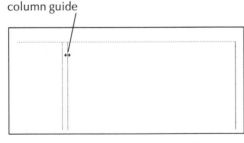

Figure 29 *Drag the column guide to create unequal width columns.*

Defining Columns

Quick and Easy Work Habits

■ PageMaker's default document configuration will probably work for many of the documents you're likely to design. When this is the case, simply start PageMaker and press **Ctrl+N** and Return. PageMaker will immediately display a new document page, ready for your design ideas.

■ If you will be working with a different format for documents, consider changing the default settings in the Document Setup dialog box. Simply start PageMaker, and without creating a new document, or opening an existing document, choose the Document Setup command on the File menu. In the Document Setup dialog box, make changes to accommodate the documents you want to create. Then you can use the **Ctrl+N** shortcut described above.

■ Remember, if you have an existing PageMaker document that is similar to one you want to define, simply save that document with a new name, open it and use it as the basis for your new document. To do so, use the Save As command on the File menu.

■ While it is possible to change the page size or margin values after you have started working on a new document, doing so may shift text and graphics unexpectedly. It's best to make those decisions when you create a new document, and stick to them.

Working with Text

VIRTUALLY ALL DESKTOP PUBLISHING software handles text on the page in a similar way: Before you can begin typing, you must first draw some sort of text box on the page and then type text in the box. PageMaker handles adding text on the page by surrounding it in one or more hidden text blocks. There is no awkward text box to draw—simply click the Text tool in a blank area of the page (outside an existing text block), and PageMaker automatically creates a new text block. When you type, PageMaker expands the depth of the block to accommodate your words.

To see a text block, choose the Pointer tool in the toolbox, and click anywhere in the text. You will see the boundaries of the selected block **(Figure 1)** with sizing handles and what PageMaker calls window shade handles. Once selected with the Pointer tool, you can:

- Move the text block—by clicking anywhere in the block other than on a sizing or window shade handle, and dragging the block to a new position.

- Re-size the text block—by clicking a sizing handle and dragging diagonally to make the block wider or narrower. Re-sizing the block doesn't change the size of the text, just the block.

- Readjust the text block—by clicking the top window shade handle and dragging up or down to adjust the starting point for the first line **(Figure 2)**.

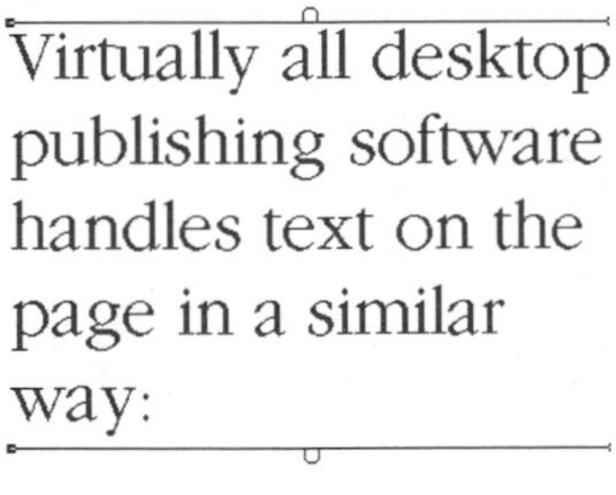

Virtually all desktop publishing software handles text on the page in a similar way:

Figure 1 *Text block showing window shade handles at top and bottom, and sizing handles at the four corners.*

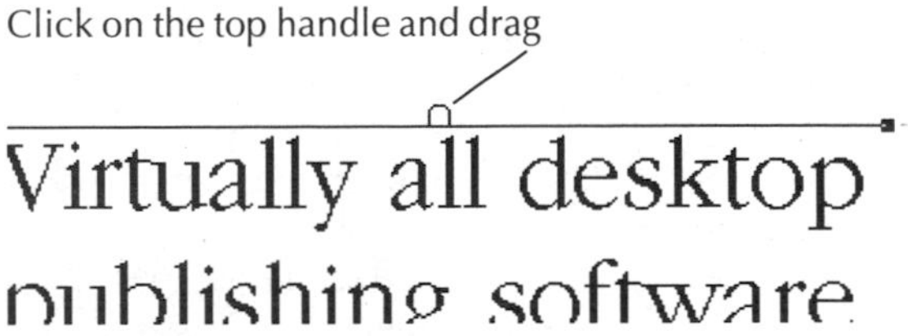

Click on the top handle and drag

Virtually all desktop publishing software

Figure 2 *Use the top handle to shift the first line up or down on the page.*

Introduction

Typing with the Text Tool

It's easy to add text to your document pages in PageMaker. Just select the Text tool. Click on the page and begin typing. PageMaker automatically creates a text block one line deep and extends the width of the block until it encounters another text block or the page margins. Typing just one letter results in an extremely wide text block. It's easy to see that the unusually wide blocks can get in the way of other text and graphics **(Figure 3)**.

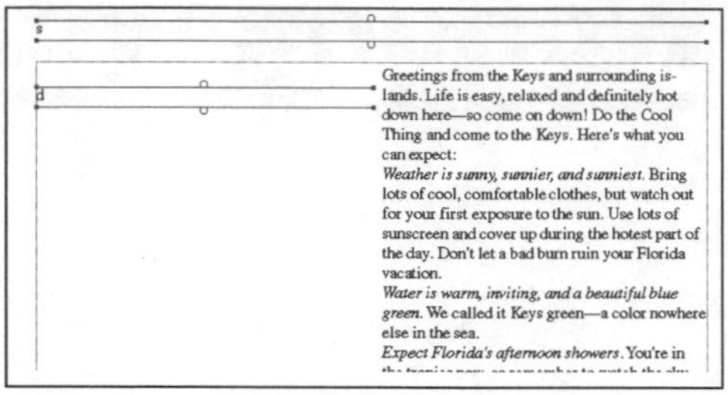

To prevent overly wide blocks, *drag out* a text block, and then begin typing. Here's how:

1 Select the Text tool in the toolbox. Position the Text tool insertion point where you want the upper left-hand corner of the text block.

2 Press and hold down the mouse button, and drag the text insertion point to the right and down. As you drag you will see a rectangular boundary display, indicating the size of the text block **(Figure 4)**.

3 When you get the size text block you want, release the mouse button. Now, without clicking the mouse again, begin typing **(Figure 5)**.

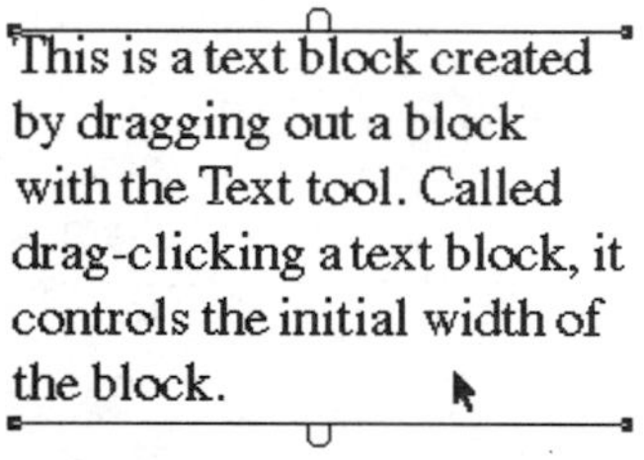

Tips

▪ If you drag out a text block and decide it isn't in the right position; just drag out a new text block. PageMaker will ignore any empty text blocks.

▪ If you're not sure where you want a particular text block to go, you can always drag out a block on the pasteboard, add the text and keep it for later use. When it comes time to add the block to your document, just click and drag it onto the page, and position it where you want **(Figure 6)**.

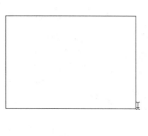

Figure 3 *Text blocks naturally extend their width until they encounter a margin or another text block.*

Figure 4 *As you drag out a text block, PageMaker displays a border showing the size of the block.*

This is a text block created by dragging out a block with the Text tool. Called drag-clicking a text block, it controls the initial width of the block.

Figure 5 *Type in the dragged-out text block and the words will wrap to the next line based on the width you set.*

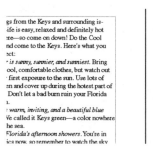

Figure 6 *The block to the right remains on the pasteboard until needed.*

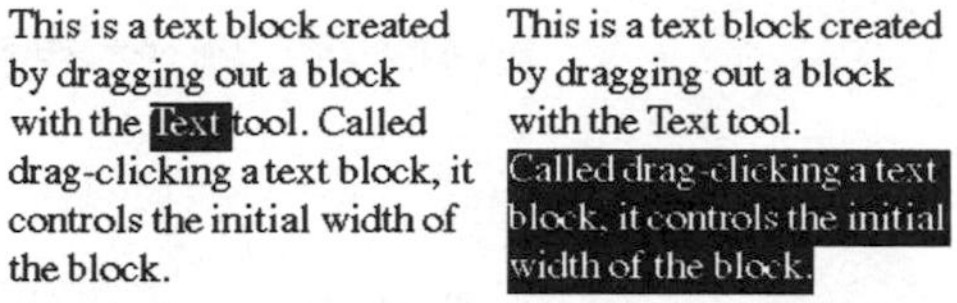

This is a text block created by dragging out a block with the [Text] tool. Called drag-clicking a text block, it controls the initial width of the block.

This is a text block created by dragging out a block with the Text tool. Called drag-clicking a text block, it controls the initial width of the block.

Figure 7 *Double-click any word to highlight the word (left), or triple-click in any paragraph to highlight the paragraph (right).*

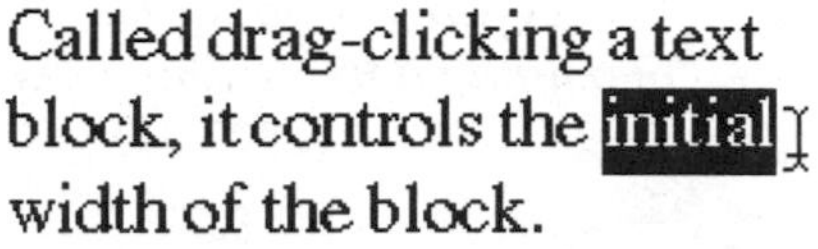

Called drag-clicking a text block, it controls the [initial] width of the block.

Figure 8 *You can highlight specific text by clicking and swiping the text insertion point through the characters you want highlighted.*

Highlighting Vs. Selecting Text

The terms highlight text and select text mean very different things to PageMaker. Highlighting is done with the Text tool; selecting is handled by a click of the Pointer tool. Selecting text chooses the whole text block—highlighting text marks only the text you want. To make changes to text already typed, you must first highlight it with the Text tool.

1 Choose the Text tool from the toolbox and move the insertion point over the text you want to highlight.

2 Double-click any single word to highlight it. Triple-click anywhere in a paragraph to highlight the entire paragraph **(Figure 7)**.

To highlight specific text, swipe with the insertion point.

3 First position the insertion point before the first character to be highlighted.

4 Press and hold down the mouse button, while dragging the insertion point across the text you want. As you drag the text will be highlighted **(Figure 8)**. Release the button when you're through.

Tip

■ Don't use the Backspace or Delete keys to change more than a few characters. Instead, to change text you've already typed, highlight and simply type the changes which will replace the highlighted text.

Highlighting and Selecting Text

Choosing the Best View

PageMaker offers you many perspectives of your work, from viewing the entire pasteboard, to a one-to-one actual size view, up to an 800% enlargement. For basic typing, the 100% (actual size) view gives you the best look at your work. To reduce or enlarge the page view, follow these steps:

1 Open the Layout menu and choose the View command **(Figure 9)**.

2 In the View submenu **(Figure 10)**, choose the perspective that best fits your needs.

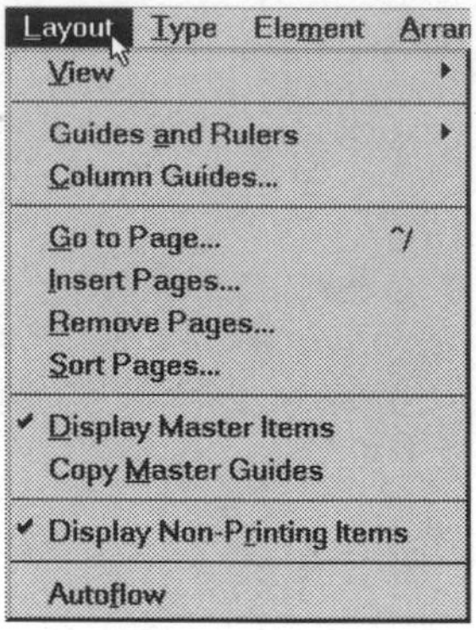

Tips

■ A quick shortcut to the Fit in Window view is **Ctrl+0** (the number 0, not the letter O).

■ Shortcuts to Actual Size (100%) and 200% are **Ctrl+1** and **Ctrl+2** respectively.

■ When you enlarge the page to see a specific area, such as a particular text block or graphic, select or highlight the area first, then choose the new view. PageMaker will magnify the page the amount you request and display the selected or highlighted area (saves you from having to scroll around on the giant page).

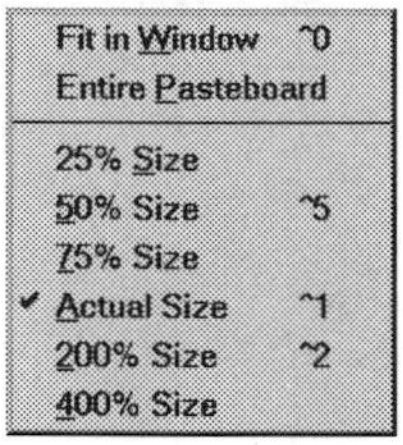

Changing Views

Figure 9 *Choose the View command on the Layout menu.*

Figure 10 *Choose the size reduction or magnification from the menu.*

Figure 11 *Use the Magnify tool to quickly change the views of your work.*

Figure 12 *Hold down the Control key to change the Magnifying tool's plus sign to a minus sign, and reduce instead of magnify the view.*

Using the Magnify Tool

Here's just the thing for a quick magnification or reduction. The Magnify tool lets you enlarge in smaller increments than the View submenu. Each time you click the tool on a document page, you get a little bit closer to your work—all the way up to 400%. Here's how to use the tool:

1 Choose the Magnify tool in the toolbox **(Figure 11)**, scroll to the area of the page you want to enlarge and click the mouse button. Your view of the page will grow each time you click.

2 To reduce the page view, hold down the Control key and click the mouse. Notice when you press Control the default Plus sign in the tool changes to a minus sign **(Figure 12)**.

Tip

▉ Here's how to enlarge your work to 800%. Even though 400% is the most you can magnify with either the Magnify tool or the View submenu, hold down the Control key and the Spacebar and click the mouse. The view will increase to a full 800%!

Magnify Tool

Changing the Width of Text Blocks

To change the length of text lines (called the *measure* of the line), use the left or right sizing handles.

1   Choose the Pointer tool in the toolbox and click the text block whose width you want to adjust.

2   Position the pointer over the lower right sizing handle **(Figure 13)**, press and hold down the mouse button.

3   Drag the sizing handle inward to shorten the measure. Then drag the handle down slightly to accommodate a deeper text block, necessitated by the narrower width. Note that dragging the right sizing handle in or out to change the block's width doesn't change its position on the document page, but only its width.

4   Now your text block might look like **Figure 14**.

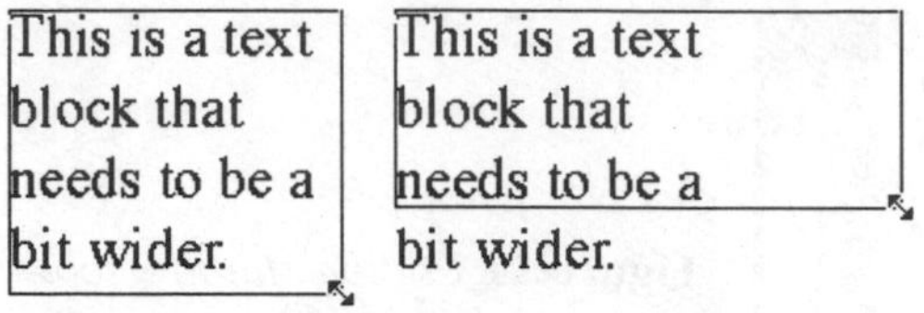

This is a text block that needs to be a bit wider. | This is a text block that needs to be a

Figure 13 *To widen the text block on the left, click the lower right sizing handle and drag to the right (like the example on the right); the text will reflow to fill the extra width.*

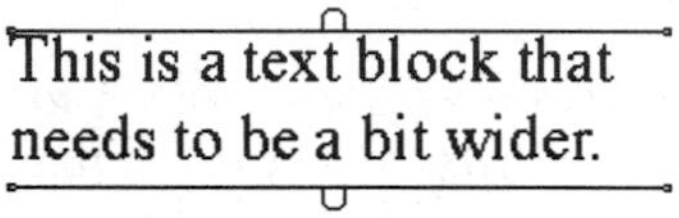

This is a text block that needs to be a bit wider.

Figure 14 *The wider text block with text reflowed.*

Adjusting Text Block Window Shades

PageMaker indicates how text is connected across text blocks (called *text threading* in PageMaker lingo) by different symbols in the top and bottom window shade handles. To see the window shade handles, click the text block with the Pointer tool.

This is a text block that

needs to be a bit wider.

This is a text block that

This is a text block that

- **Empty handle**—at the top means the beginning of a text block. An empty handle at the bottom means there is no more text in the text block. A text block with empty handles means there is no text threaded from or to another block and all the text is placed on the page.

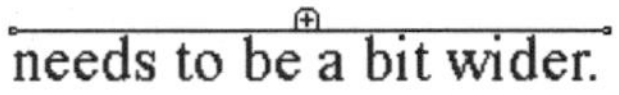

- **Plus sign in top handle**—means text from a previous text block is threaded to this text block.

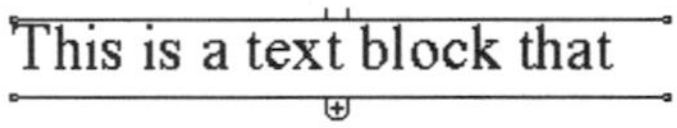

- **Plus sign in bottom handle**—means text in the block is threaded to another text block.

- **Red arrow in bottom handle**—means the text block contains additional text not yet placed on the page or threaded to the text in the current text block.

To place the text, either:

- Drag the window shade down to reveal the remaining text (when all the text is displayed the handle will be empty); or

- Click the handle and the cursor arrow will change to a loaded text icon **(Figure 15)**. Position the cursor where you want the new text block, click and drag out a new text block, and the text will flow into the text block.

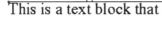

Figure 15 *Loaded text icon means a click of the mouse will add text at the mouse pointer's position (cancel by clicking any tool in the toolbox).*

Importing Text from a Word Processor

If you choose to do the majority of writing for a document in your favorite word processor, PageMaker can probably import the text without any trouble. PageMaker comes with a wide variety of import filters (which you selected and installed when you installed PageMaker). Here's how to import text:

1 Using any tool in PageMaker's toolbox, click open the File menu and choose the Place command **(Figure 16)**.

2 The Place dialog box **(Figure 17)** is used to import (or *place*, as PageMaker calls it) text and graphics into your documents. Use the list box to locate the file you want to import.

3 Click OK to import the text. In a moment PageMaker will display a loaded text icon. Now, drag place the text like this:

4 Position the icon in the upper left corner where you want the text block to begin. Then, press and hold down the mouse button, while you drag out the text block **(Figure 18)**.

5 When the outlined text block is sized and positioned properly, release the mouse button to fill the block with text. If the bottom window shade handle contains a red arrow, click and drag out another text block to place the remaining text.

Figure 16 *Choose the Place command on the File menu.*

Find the file you want to import here

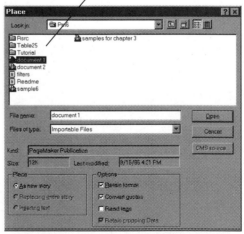

Figure 18 *Drag-placing text lets you control the exact size of the text block.*

Figure 17 *Use the Place dialog box to import text and graphics.*

Importing Text

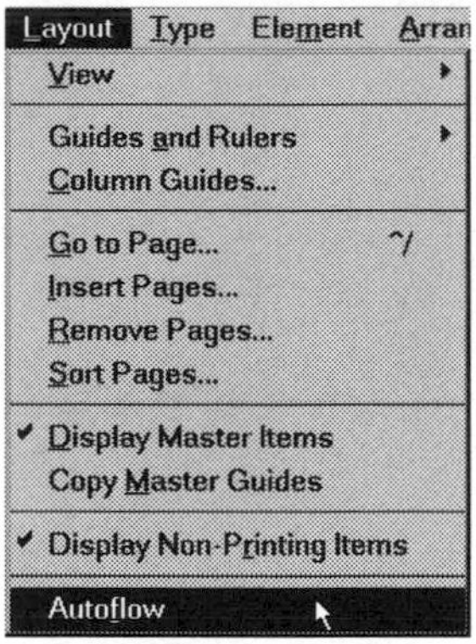

Figure 19 *Choose the Autoflow command on the Layout menu.*

Controlling the Page Flow When Placing Text

A large amount of text may fill up several pages of text—more than is convenient to drag place across the multiple pages of your document. When working with large text files, use PageMaker's autoflow feature. When enabled, PageMaker will create as many pages as necessary to hold the text, and the placed text will be automatically added to the pages.

1 Choose the Layout menu **(Figure 19)**.

2 The Autoflow command is enabled (operational) when a check mark is displayed beside it.

3 If the check mark isn't present, choose the command to add the check mark.

Tip

■ You can tell whether Autoflow is on or off by the look of the loaded text cursor when you are ready to place text on the page **(Figure 20)**.

Figure 20 *When Autoflow is off the loaded text icon looks like the left-hand example; the right hand example is when Autoflow is activated.*

Importing Text

Story Editor

Editing with the Story Editor

When editing larger amounts of text, use PageMaker's own word processor, called the *story editor*. In the story editor you see your text not laid out and composed, but as lines of text—easy to read and easy to correct. There is a spell checker available, as well as PageMaker's Find and Change commands. To edit your text in the story editor:

1 Choose the Text tool from the toolbox and click the insertion point in the text you wish to edit.

2 Open the Edit menu and choose the Edit Story command **(Figure 21)**. In a moment you will see your text displayed in the story editor **(Figure 22)**.

3 You can close the story editor and return to your document in the document editor by opening the Story menu and choosing **Close story**.

Tips

■ A quick shortcut to the story editor is to press **Ctrl+E**. Press the shortcut again to move back to the document editor.

■ To display hard returns and spaces between words, open the Story menu and choose the **Display ¶** command. Hard returns are indicated by the paragraph symbol, while spaces are shown by very faint dots.

■ To see the names of styles assigned to text, open the Story menu and choose the **Display Style Names** command. Style names will be indicated in the left margin **(Figure 23)**.

■ You can change the type style and size of text displayed in the story editor with the Preferences dialog box. Simply open the File menu and choose **Preferences**. Then click the **More** button and go to the Story editor area of the dialog box.

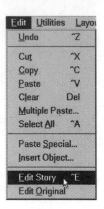

Figure 21 *Choose the Edit Story command on the Edit menu.*

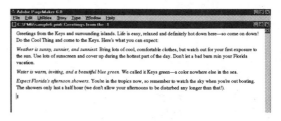

Figure 22 *Story editor displays text like a word processor, making it easier to type and edit copy.*

Figure 23 *Story editor showing style names in left margin.*

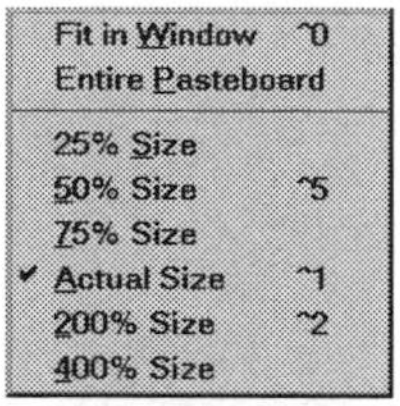

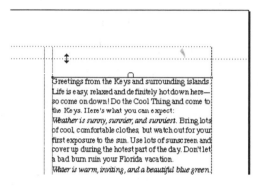

Figure 24 *Choose the view you want with the View submenu.*

Greetings from the Keys and surrounding islands! Life is easy, relaxed and definitely hot down here— so come on down! Do the Cool Thing and come to the Keys. Here's what you can expect:
Weather is sunny, sunnier, and sunniest. Bring lots of cool, comfortable clothes, but watch out for your first exposure to the sun. Use lots of sunscreen and cover up during the hotest part of the day. Don't let a bad burn ruin your Florida vacation.
Water is warm, inviting, and a beautiful blue green.

Figure 25 *Use a horizontal guide to set the top column positions on the page.*

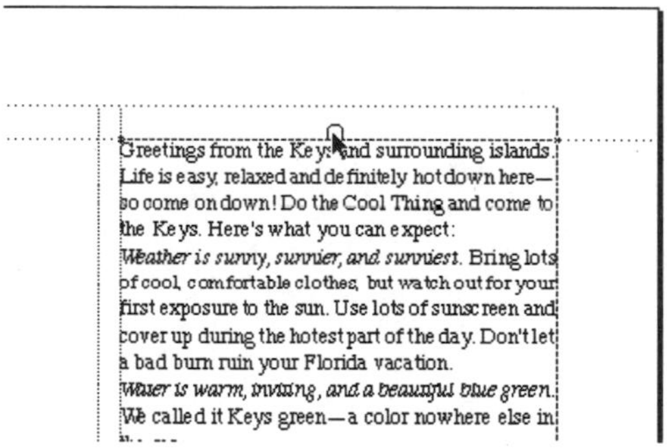

Greetings from the Keys and surrounding islands! Life is easy, relaxed and definitely hot down here— so come on down! Do the Cool Thing and come to the Keys. Here's what you can expect:
Weather is sunny, sunnier, and sunniest. Bring lots of cool, comfortable clothes, but watch out for your first exposure to the sun. Use lots of sunscreen and cover up during the hotest part of the day. Don't let a bad burn ruin your Florida vacation.
Water is warm, inviting, and a beautiful blue green. We called it Keys green—a color nowhere else in

Figure 26 *Now, click the top handle and drag the column up to "snap to" the guide you set.*

Positioning Text Blocks

In multiple column designs, you may need to manually adjust the tops of text blocks to make them even and aligned correctly. Here's how:

1 Choose a view size large enough to make fine adjustments to the top of the text blocks. To change views, open the Layout menu and choose the View submenu **(Figure 24)**. Then select the magnification you want.

2 Pull a guide out of the top ruler and adjust it on the page as the controlling guide for the text blocks **(Figure 25)**.

3 Now, click each text block with the Pointer tool, click the top window shade handle and drag it up to snap to the guide **(Figure 26)**. (If the Snap To feature is not enabled, use the shortcut **Ctrl+5** to toggle it on.)

Tip

■ To even up columns on the page you can also use the Balance Columns plugin. First, Shift+click the number of columns on the page that you want to balance. Then, click open the Utilities menu and choose the PageMaker Plugins submenu. Choose Balance Columns. PageMaker will show you the Balance Columns dialog box to specify how you want the columns adjusted. Click OK to have the plug-in balance the columns for you.

Aligning Text Blocks

Connecting Text Blocks

If you have two different text blocks and wish to combine them into a single text block:

1 Highlight the text in the text block you want to add to another text block and choose **Cut** from the Edit menu **(Figure 27)**.

2 The highlighted text will disappear. Now click the insertion point in the text block where you want to add the text and choose **Paste** from the Edit menu.

Figure 27 *Choose the Cut command from the Edit menu.*

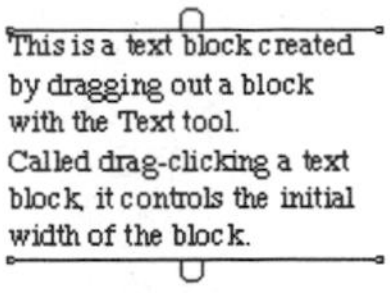

This is a text block created
by dragging out a block
with the Text tool.
Called drag-clicking a text
block, it controls the initial
width of the block.

Figure 28 *Select the text block with the Pointer tool.*

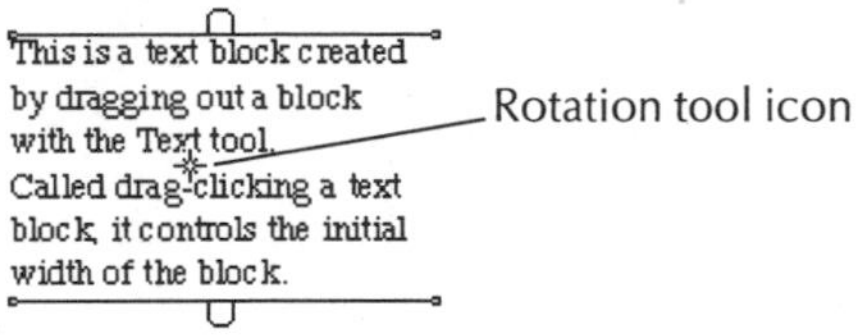

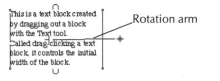

This is a text block created
by dragging out a block
with the Text tool.
Called drag-clicking a text
block, it controls the initial
width of the block.

— Rotation tool icon

Figure 29 *Position Rotation tool icon in center of text block.*

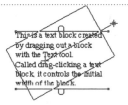

This is a text block created
by dragging out a block
with the Text tool.
Called drag-clicking a text
block, it controls the initial
width of the block.

Rotation arm

Figure 30 *Click and drag a rotation arm to the right.*

This is a text block created
by dragging out a block
with the Text tool.
Called drag-clicking a text
block, it controls the initial
width of the block.

Figure 31 *Now, drag the arm up or down to rotate the text block.*

45°
0°

Figure 32 *Enter the degrees of rotation in the Control palette text box, and press Enter.*

Figure 33 *Use the Control palette's nudge buttons to rotate the selected text block.*

Rotating Text

Text blocks can be rotated in any of 360 degrees, clockwise or counterclockwise, using either the Rotation tool or the Control palette.

1 Choose the Pointer tool from the toolbox and click the text block you want to rotate **(Figure 28)**.

2 To rotate using the Rotation tool, select the tool from the toolbox, and position the tool's icon over the center of the text box **(Figure 29)**.

3 Depress the mouse button and drag the icon to the right side of the text block. The Rotation tool will display a rotation arm **(Figure 30)**.

4 Now, while continuing to press the mouse button, move the rotation arm clockwise or counterclockwise to rotate the text block **(Figure 31)**.

To rotate the text block using the Control palette:

1 Select the Pointer tool from the toolbox and select the text block you want to rotate.

2 If the Control palette isn't displayed, choose the Window menu and click the Control palette command.

3 Enter the number of degrees of rotation in the rotation text box **(Figure 32)** and press Return. Enter a positive number up to 360 to rotate counterclockwise, or a negative number to rotate clockwise.

4 Alternately, you can use the up or down rotation nudge buttons **(Figure 33)**. Note that the nudge up button rotates counterclockwise, and the nudge down button rotates clockwise.

Rotating Text Blocks

Quick and Easy Work Habits

Quick Work Tips

- If you click a red window shade handle to place text, and you decide not to place it just yet, cancel by clicking any other tool in PageMaker's toolbox.

- The mark of a true amateur using PageMaker is text blocks considerably wider than the text width. The extra wide text blocks overlap other elements and just get in the way. Control the width of text blocks by dragging out just the width you need.

- To open the Place dialog box use the shortcut **Ctrl+D**.

- To toggle back and forth between the layout editor (where you see your laid out pages) and the story editor (PageMaker's word processor), press the shortcut **Ctrl+E**.

- To see what your text will look like in a variety of fonts, highlight the text with the Text tool, and use the Control palette to apply fonts to the highlighted text. (See Chapter 5 to learn more about using the Control palette to specify type.)

- To see all the text blocks on the page (and all graphic elements as well), open the Edit menu and choose the Select All command. Then you can select just the block you want.

- To select more than one text block, choose the Pointer tool, and click the first text block you want to select. Then, hold down the Shift key and click on the remaining text blocks (or graphic elements). You can move all selected text blocks at once by then clicking on any single block and dragging—all selected blocks will tag along in their same, relative position.

Formatting Paragraphs 4

PARAGRAPHS ARE BASIC BUILDING blocks of almost any document. PageMaker's paragraph specifications make quick and easy work to get just the look you want. This chapter covers the basics of formatting text into paragraphs. You will learn:

- How paragraphs are aligned to the edges of the margins that define them;

- How indents and tabs are defined and used;

- How PageMaker controls splitting paragraphs across page breaks;

- How PageMaker hyphenates words that would normally extend past the right margin; and

- How to define automatic lines that can be added above or below paragraphs.

PageMaker's paragraph specifications are easy to make and simple to modify. Simply click the Text tool insertion point anywhere in the paragraph you want to change, and make the needed changes. The most valuable asset in specifying paragraphs is assigning the specifications to a paragraph style. Then to modify a number of paragraphs at the same time, simply modify the style. Styles are explained in Chapter 7.

Paragraph Alignment

Aligning Text in Paragraphs

When you begin adding text in text blocks, you will see PageMaker's default paragraph alignment—flush left when it is first installed. PageMaker gives you alignment choices of:

- **Align left**—the left edge of the text block is even; the right edge is ragged **(Figure 1)**.

- **Align right**—the right side of the text block is even and the left edge is ragged **(Figure 2)**.

- **Align center**—each line is centered in the text block and both sides of the text block are ragged **(Figure 3)**.

- **Justify**—both sides of the text block are even, and spacing between letters and words is varied to compensate for different line lengths **(Figure 4)**.

- **Force justify**—used to force a short line length to be evenly spread the full width of the text block **(Figure 5)**.

Tip

- How to change the default alignment setting: If you know you want a paragraph alignment different from PageMaker's current default alignment, it's easy to create a new default setting. Simply choose the Alignment command on the Type menu with all documents closed. In the Alignment submenu, choose the default alignment you want.

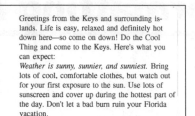

Greetings from the Keys and surrounding islands. Life is easy, relaxed and definitely hot down here—so come on down! Do the Cool Thing and come to the Keys. Here's what you can expect: *Weather is sunny, sunnier, and sunniest.* Bring lots of cool, comfortable clothes, but watch out for your first exposure to the sun. Use lots of sunscreen and cover up during the hottest part of the day. Don't let a bad burn ruin your Florida vacation.

Figure 1 *Left-aligned text.*

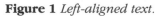

Greetings from the Keys and surrounding islands. Life is easy, relaxed and definitely hot down here—so come on down! Do the Cool Thing and come to the Keys. Here's what you can expect: *Weather is sunny, sunnier, and sunniest.* Bring lots of cool, comfortable clothes, but watch out for your first exposure to the sun. Use lots of sunscreen and cover up during the hottest part of the day. Don't let a bad burn ruin your Florida vacation.

Figure 2 *Right-aligned text*

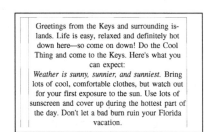

Greetings from the Keys and surrounding islands. Life is easy, relaxed and definitely hot down here—so come on down! Do the Cool Thing and come to the Keys. Here's what you can expect: *Weather is sunny, sunnier, and sunniest.* Bring lots of cool, comfortable clothes, but watch out for your first exposure to the sun. Use lots of sunscreen and cover up during the hottest part of the day. Don't let a bad burn ruin your Florida vacation.

Figure 3 *Centered text.*

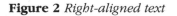

Greetings from the Keys and surrounding islands. Life is easy, relaxed and definitely hot down here—so come on down! Do the Cool Thing and come to the Keys. Here's what you can expect: *Weather is sunny, sunnier, and sunniest.* Bring lots of cool, comfortable clothes, but watch out for your first exposure to the sun. Use lots of sunscreen and cover up during the hottest part of the day. Don't let a bad burn ruin your Florida vacation.

Figure 4 *Justified text.*

Greetings from the Keys and surrounding islands. Life is easy, relaxed and definitely hot down here—so come on down! Do the Cool Thing and come to the Keys. Here's what you can expect: *Weather is sunny, sunnier, and sunniest.* Bring lots of cool, comfortable clothes, but watch out for your first exposure to the sun. Use lots of sunscreen and cover up during the hottest part of the day. Don't let a bad burn ruin your Florida vacation.

Figure 5 *Force-justified text (note the last line compared with Figure 4).*

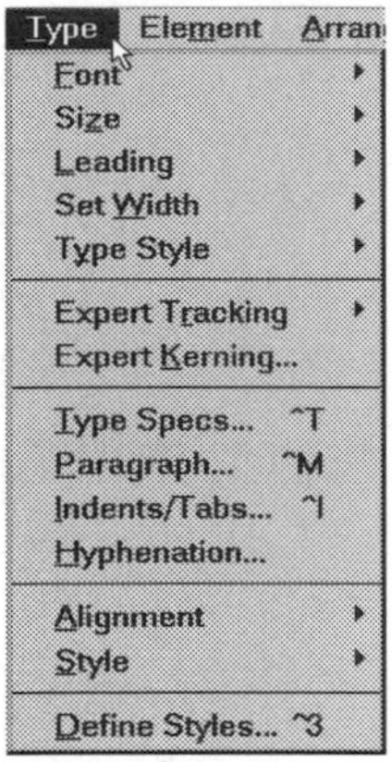

Type	Element	Arran
Font	▶
Size	▶
Leading	▶
Set Width	▶
Type Style	▶
Expert Tracking	▶
Expert Kerning...	
Type Specs...	^T
Paragraph...	^M
Indents/Tabs...	^I
Hyphenation...	
Alignment	▶
Style	▶
Define Styles...	^3

Figure 6 *Choose the Alignment command on the Type menu.*

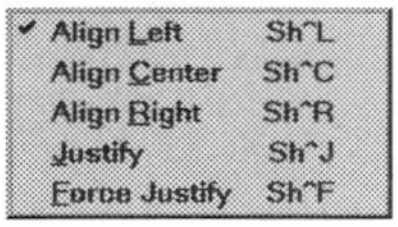

Align Left	Sh^L
Align Center	Sh^C
Align Right	Sh^R
Justify	Sh^J
Force Justify	Sh^F

Figure 7 *Choose the alignment you want from the submenu.*

Specifying Paragraph Alignment

To choose an alignment setting:

1 Select the Text tool and click on the page where you want the text block.

2 Click open the Type menu and choose the Alignment command **(Figure 6)**. You will see the Alignment submenu open **(Figure 7)**.

3 Choose the alignment you want from the submenu.

4 Begin typing. The text will be formatted to the alignment you selected.

If you click open another text block, PageMaker will assume its default alignment setting.

Paragraph Alignment

Setting Alignment as a Paragraph Specification

Another way of choosing an initial alignment setting for a text block is by using the Paragraph Specifications dialog box. Any changes made to the dialog box before you begin typing affect all paragraphs in the text block. Here's how:

1 Choose the Text tool and click on the page where you want the text block.

2 Click open the Type menu and choose the Paragraph command **(Figure 8)**.

3 PageMaker will open the Paragraph Specifications dialog box **(Figure 9)**. Click open the Alignment list box **(Figure 10)** and choose the alignment you want.

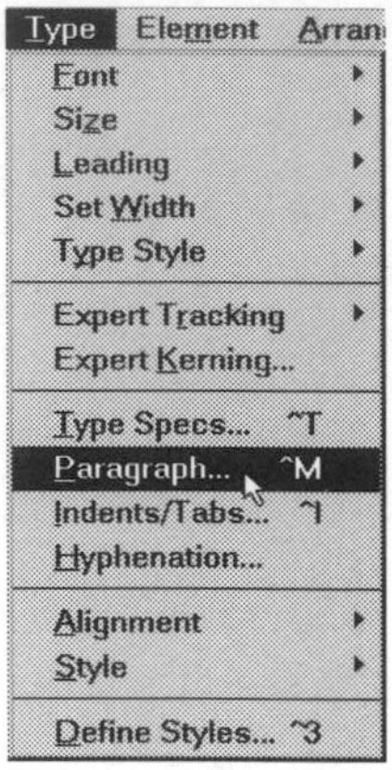

Tips

■ A quick way to open the Paragraph Specifications dialog box is to use the shortcut **Ctrl+M**.

■ Use styles to save time in formatting different paragraphs with different alignment styles. Chapter 7 explains all about styles.

Figure 8 *Choose the Paragraph command on the Type menu.*

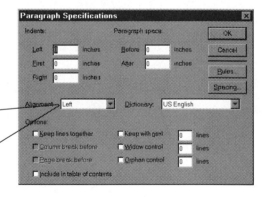

Figure 9 *Paragraph Specifications dialog box.*

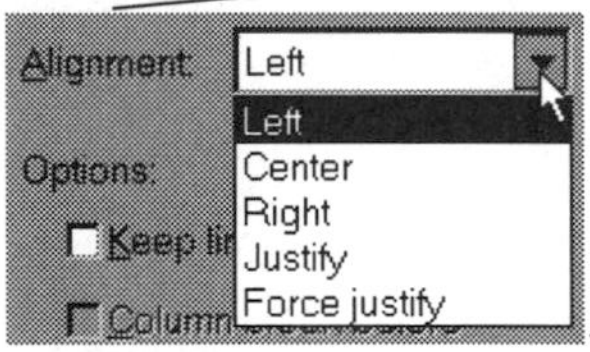

Figure 10 *Choose the alignment in the Alignment list box.*

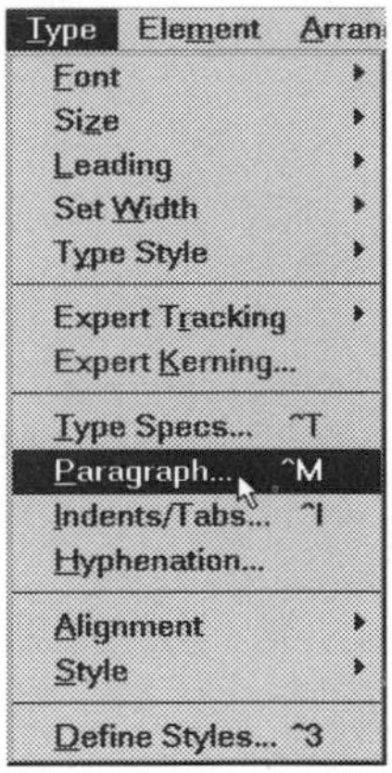

Figure 11 *Choose the Paragraph command from the Type menu.*

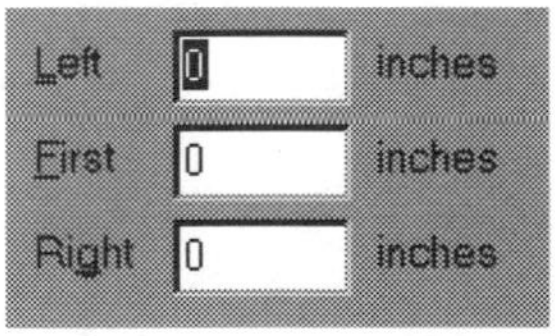

About Indents

PageMaker offers several different indent formats for paragraphs:

- **Left indent**—moves the left edge of all lines in the paragraph to the right.

- **First indent**—moves only the left edge of the first line of the paragraph to the right.

- **Right indent**—moves the right edge of all lines in the paragraph to the left.

- **Hanging indent**—moves the left edge of the first line to the left so that it hangs out over the paragraph.

Indents are controlled by the Paragraph Specifications dialog box. Let's take a look:

1. To specify an indent for a new text block, choose the Text tool and click on the page where you want the text block. To create or change an indent for an existing paragraph, first highlight the paragraph.

2. Next, click open the Type menu and choose the Paragraph command **(Figure 11)**. Indents are controlled by the Indents area of the Paragraph Specifications dialog box **(Figure 12)**.

3. Enter values in the three text boxes to set the type of indent you want.

Figure 12 *Use the Left, First and Right text boxes to control indents.*

Paragraph Alignment

Setting Left Indents

1 Click open the Type menu and choose Paragraph to open the Paragraph Specifications dialog box **(Figure 13)**.

2 In the Indents area, enter the amount in the **Left** text box you want to indent the left edge of your paragraph **(Figure 14)**.

3 Click OK to return to your document. The left-indented paragraph will look like **(Figure 15)**.

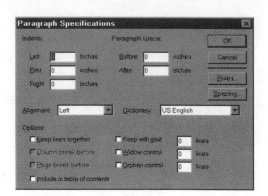

Figure 13 *Open the Paragraph Specifications dialog box.*

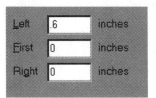

Figure 14 *Entering the value to create a left-indented paragraph.*

Greetings from the Keys and surrounding islands. Life is easy, relaxed and definitely hot down here— so come on down! Do the Cool Thing and come to the Keys. Here's what you can expect:

Weather is sunny, sunnier, and sunniest. Bring lots of cool, comfortable clothes, but watch out

Figure 15 *Top paragraph is left indented.*

Paragraph Alignment

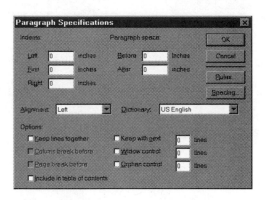

Figure 16 *Paragraph Specifications dialog box.*

Setting Right Indents

1 Click open the Type menu and choose Paragraph to open the Paragraph Specifications dialog box **(Figure 16)**.

2 In the Indents area, enter the amount in the Right text box you want to indent the right edge of your paragraph from the right margin **(Figure 17)**.

3 Click OK to return to your document. The right-indented paragraph will look like **(Figure 18)**.

Left	0	inches
First	0	inches
Right	0.6	inches

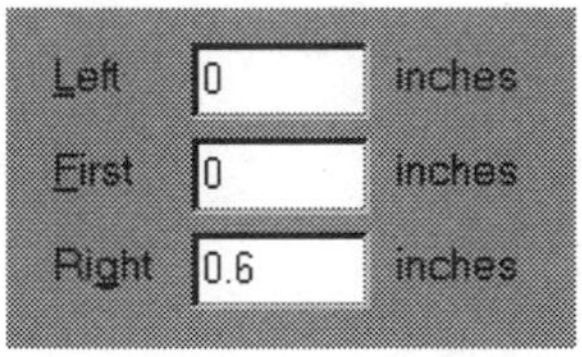

Figure 17 *Entering the value to create a right-indented paragraph.*

Greetings from the Keys and surrounding islands. Life is easy, relaxed and definitely hot down here— so come on down! Do the Cool Thing and come to the Keys. Here's what you can expect: Weather is sunny, sunnier, and sunniest. Bring lots of cool, comfortable clothes, but watch out

Figure 18 *Top paragraph is right indented.*

Paragraph Alignment

Setting First Line Indents

1 Click open the Type menu and choose Paragraph to open the Paragraph Specifications dialog box **(Figure 19)**.

2 In the Indents area, enter the amount in the First text box to indent the first line of your paragraph **(Figure 20)**.

3 Click OK. The paragraph will look like **(Figure 21)**.

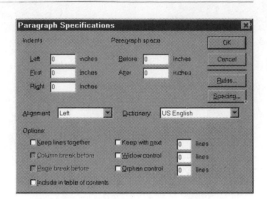

Figure 19 *Paragraph Specifications dialog box.*

Left	0	inches
First	0.5	inches
Right	0	inches

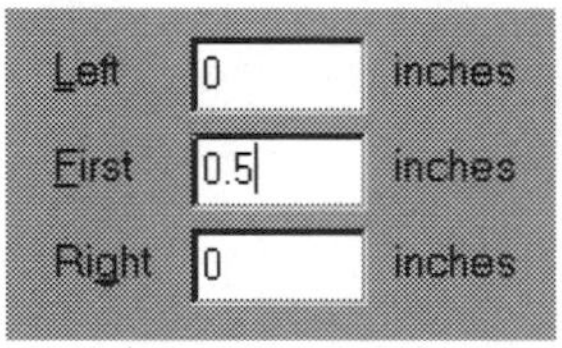

Figure 20 *Entering the value to create a first line-indented paragraph.*

Paragraph Alignment

> Greetings from the Keys and surrounding islands. Life is easy, relaxed and definitely hot down here—so come on down! Do the Cool Thing and come to the Keys. Here's what you can expect:
> Weather is sunny, sunnier, and sunniest. Bring lots of cool, comfortable clothes, but watch out for your first exposure to the sun. Use lots of sunscreen and cover up

Figure 21 *Top paragraph has a first line indent.*

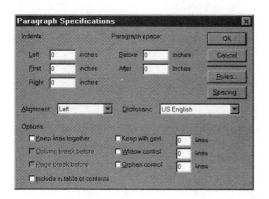

Figure 22 *Paragraph Specifications dialog box.*

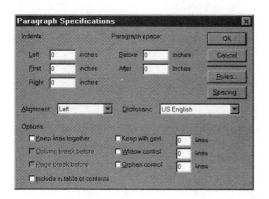

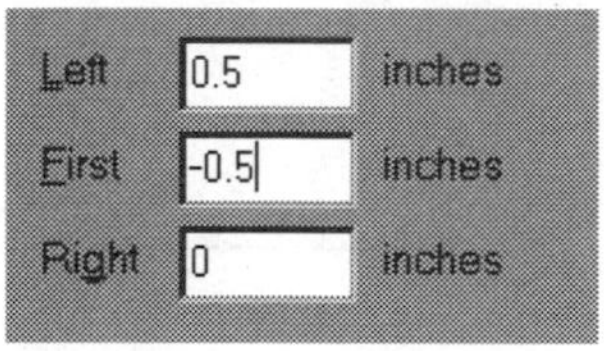

Figure 23 *Entering the values to create a hanging indent.*

Greetings from the Keys and surrounding islands. Life is easy, relaxed and definitely hot down here—so come on down! Do the Cool Thing and come to the Keys. Here's what you can expect: Weather is sunny, sunnier, and sunniest. Bring lots of cool, comfortable clothes, but watch out for your first exposure to the sun. Use

Setting Hanging Indents

Hanging indents are sort of the opposite of first line indents; except in this case every line but the first is indented.

1 Open the Paragraph Specifications dialog box **(Figure 22)**.

2 Set up a left indent by entering a value in the Left text box to move the left edge of the paragraph to the right.

3 Then, enter the same value in the First text box, as a negative number (put a minus sign in front of the value). In other words, if you entered .5 in the Left text to create a .5-inch left indent, enter -.5 in the First text box **(Figure 23)**. The negative value moves the left edge of the first line back to the original left margin for the text box, creating the hanging indent. Your paragraph will look like **Figure 24**.

Figure 24 *Top paragraph has a hanging indent.*

Paragraph Alignment

Setting Tabs

Tabs are set similarly to indents. They are activated by pressing the tab key. Unfortunately PageMaker has never been known for easy tabs, which will tend to drive you crazy if you don't know a simple trick. The key to setting and managing tabs in PageMaker is to create the text entries that you want aligned with tab settings *before* making the tab settings. Here are the steps:

1 Type the entries you want tab-aligned. Press the tab key only once before each entry. At this point the entries will not be aligned **(Figure 25)**.

2 Magnify the view to at least actual size (press **Ctrl+1**).

3 Now, highlight the entries with the Text tool, and choose the Indent/Tabs command on the Type menu.

4 Use the Indent/Tabs dialog box **(Figure 26)** to set each tab. First, shift the tab ruler over to align with the width of your text box **(Figure 27)**.

5 Click the tab icon for left, right, center, or decimal aligned tabs.

6 Finally, click the mouse arrow on the ruler where you want the tab set, or type the exact position in the Position text box.

Your tabs will now be aligned, like the example in **Figure 28**.

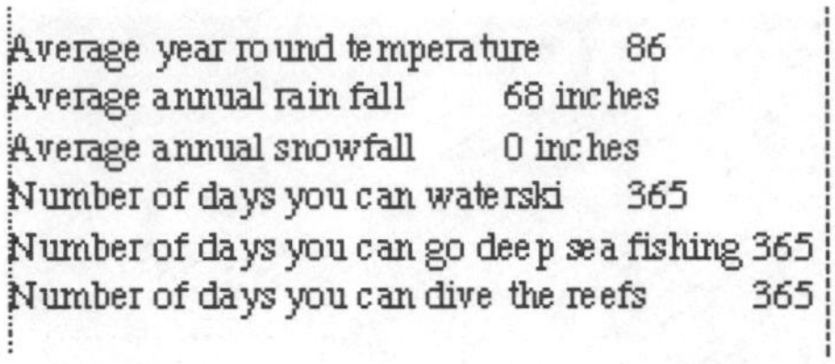

Average year round temperature   86
Average annual rain fall   68 inches
Average annual snowfall   0 inches
Number of days you can water ski   365
Number of days you can go deep sea fishing 365
Number of days you can dive the reefs   365

Figure 25 *Type the text and press the Tab key for each tab setting regardless of jumble it creates.*

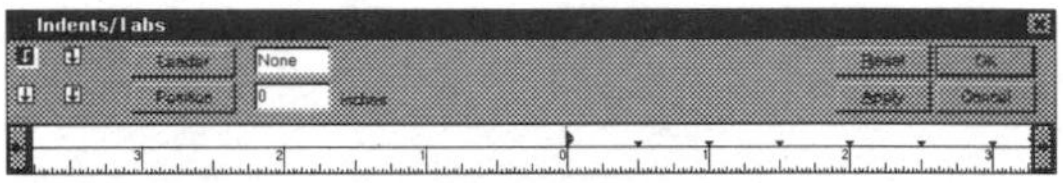

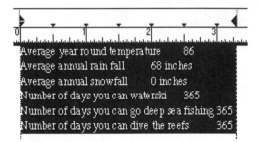

Figure 26 *Indents/Tabs dialog box.*

Average year round temperature   86
Average annual rain fall   68 inches
Average annual snowfall   0 inches
Number of days you can water ski   365
Number of days you can go deep sea fishing 365
Number of days you can dive the reefs   365

Figure 27 *Align the tab ruler with the text block, before setting tabs.*

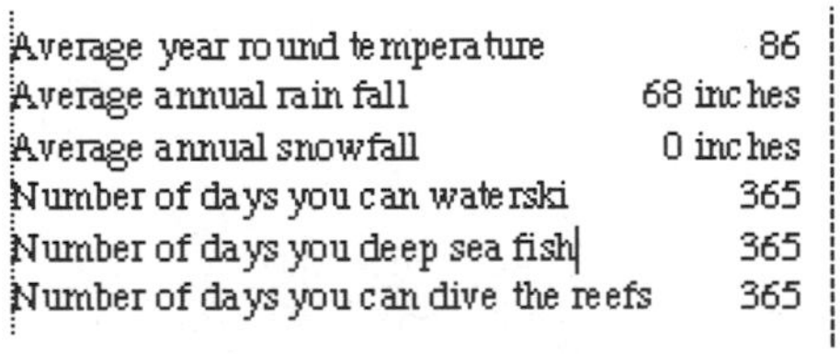

Average year round temperature   86
Average annual rain fall   68 inches
Average annual snowfall   0 inches
Number of days you can water ski   365
Number of days you deep sea fish   365
Number of days you can dive the reefs   365

Figure 28 *Now, with tabs set on the tab ruler, click OK to see the tabs aligned.*

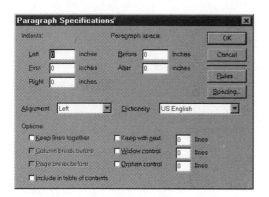

Figure 29 *Paragraph Specifications dialog box controls widowed and orphaned lines.*

Controlling Widows and Orphans

Widows and orphans are the bedraggled remnants of paragraphs that fall across page breaks. An *orphan* is the first line of a paragraph that falls at the very bottom of the page—the rest of the paragraph is pushed to the top of the next page by the page break. Likewise a *widow* is the last line of paragraph that winds up all by itself at the top of a new page—again pushed there by a page break.

Single lines, at either the top or bottom of the page, are considered bad form in page composition. Luckily PageMaker can easily control these wayward lines.

1 Click open the type menu and choose the Paragraph command.

2 PageMaker will open the Paragraph Specifications dialog box **(Figure 29)**.

3 To control widows, click the **Widow control** check box to add a check. Then enter the number of lines you want PageMaker to keep together at the top of the page. If you enter 3, for example, whenever a widow will be created, PageMaker will automatically move three lines to the next page, instead of the widowed, single line.

4 Similarly, to control orphans, click the **Orphan control** check box. Generally you will want to control both widows and orphans in the same document.

Tip

▓ You need not worry where in the document you are when you activate widow and orphan control. Once turned on, all pages are monitored for widows and orphans.

Widows and Orphans

About Hyphenation

Hyphenation is often referred to as *hyphenation and justification*, or *H&J* for short, because hyphenating words at the end of lines is especially important in justified text. Without hyphenation, justifying lines in a paragraph can create ugly gaps in letter and word spacing **(Figure 30)**. But, by allowing PageMaker to hyphenate, spacing is closed up and much more appealing to the eye **(Figure 31)**.

Hyphenation isn't only for justified paragraphs; it is just as helpful in aligned-left paragraphs, to even out the ragged-right edge of the text block **(Figure 32)**. Applying hyphenation here allows a more refined look to the paragraph **(Figure 33)**.

PageMaker controls hyphenation in either justified or unjustified paragraphs by setting a vertical zone along the right edge of the text blocks. Called the *hyphenation zone*, any word that, unhyphenated, would extend past the right edge of the zone and can be properly hyphenated, will be. The wider the zone, the less words are hyphenated; the narrower the zone, the more words PageMaker tries to hyphenate.

Because of Selective Availability, differential beacon receivers can reduce the inaccuracy of Global Positioning System receivers to a mere 10 feet.

Figure 30
Justified text without the advantage of hyphenation can result in wide spacing.

Because of Selective Availability, differential beacon receivers can reduce the inaccuracy of Global Positioning System receivers to a mere 10 feet.

Figure 31
Justified text with hyphenation greatly improves spacing problems.

Because of Selective Availability, differential beacon receivers can reduce the inaccuracy of Global Positioning System receivers to a mere 10 feet.

Figure 32
Left-aligned text without hyphenation creates an extremely ragged right margin.

Because of Selective Availability, differential beacon receivers can reduce the inaccuracy of Global Positioning System receivers to a mere 10 feet.

Figure 33
Left-aligned text with hyphenation evens out the ragged right margin.

Hyphenation

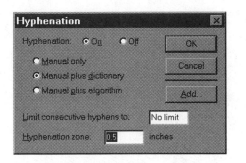

Figure 34 *Hyphenation dialog box.*

Controlling Hyphenation

1 Click open the Type menu and choose the Hyphenation command. PageMaker will open the Hyphenation dialog box **(Figure 34)**.

2 To turn on hyphenation for all the paragraphs in your document, click the **On** button.

3 Now, choose the hyphenation method you want PageMaker to use:

■ **Manual**—Each time PageMaker decides to hyphenate a word, you must decide where to add the hyphen. This is certainly the slowest form of hyphenation (and the most likely for mistakes).

■ **Manual plus dictionary**—PageMaker normally uses its spelling dictionary to see where words can be correctly hyphenated. If it can't decide, it will display a manual hyphenation dialog box for you to hyphenate the word. This is the most accurate method.

■ **Manual plus algorithm**—Instead of using its spelling dictionary, PageMaker uses special programmed logic to decide where to hyphenate words. Again, if it can't figure out the word, you will hyphenate it manually. This is the fastest method, but not very accurate.

4 PageMaker sets a default hyphenation zone of .5 inch. Change the zone to increase or decrease the number of hyphenated words.

5 To gain access to the dictionary and show PageMaker how to hyphenate a word, click **Add**.

Hyphenation

Adding Lines Above and Below Paragraphs

Besides the line tool found in PageMaker's toolbox, you can add lines as a part of the paragraph specification. Automatic lines added as a part of the paragraph can be handy if only because you don't have to draw them individually for each paragraph. Here are the steps:

1 Click open the Type menu and choose the Paragraph command to see the Paragraph Specifications dialog box **(Figure 35)**.

2 Click **Rules** to open the Paragraph Rules dialog box **(Figure 36)**.

3 Decide whether you want to add a rule (or line, same thing) above or below paragraphs. Click the appropriate check box.

4 Now, decide the thickness of the rule, its color and tint.

5 The **Options** button lets you specify the rules in relation to the top or bottom baseline for each paragraph.

Hold down the Control key and click OK to return to your document.

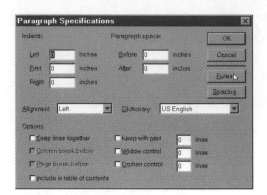

Figure 35 *Choose the Rules button in the Paragraph Specifications dialog box.*

Decide line thickness, color and tint

Click to add lines above or below

Decide width of line here

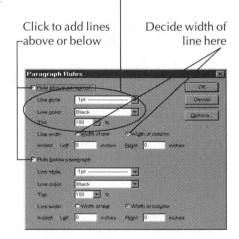

Figure 36 *Paragraph Rules dialog box lets you add lines above or below paragraphs, automatically.*

Working with the Control Palette

The Control palette gives you instant access to the settings in a number of dialog boxes. When formatting paragraphs click the paragraph view button to see paragraph-related tools **(Figure 37)**.

▓ **Alignment buttons**—use these to set paragraph alignment instead of using the Alignment submenu.

▓ **Left and Right Indent text boxes**—click and enter a value in one of these to handle indents, instead of opening the Paragraph specification dialog box.

Text view button
Paragraph view button
First-line indent   Space above paragraph

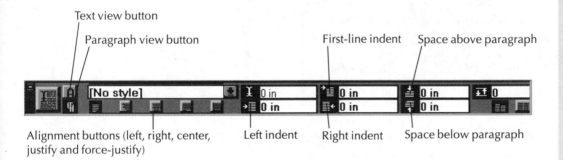

Alignment buttons (left, right, center,   Left indent   Right indent   Space below paragraph
justify and force-justify)

Figure 37 *Paragraph view of Control palette showing alignment buttons, and indent and paragraph space text boxes.*

Control Palette

Quick and Easy Work Habits

▪ Aligning paragraphs with the Alignment command is tiresome—it takes three mouse actions to change an alignment. Instead, set the alignment while you're formatting the paragraph in the Paragraph Specifications dialog box.

To change alignment after that, the easiest way is to click the text insertion point in the paragraph and use one of the following keyboard shortcuts:

Press this	To get this
Ctrl+Shift+L	Aligned Left
Ctrl+Shift+R	Aligned Right
Ctrl+Shift+C	Centered
Ctrl+Shift+J	Justified
Ctrl+Shift+F	Force Justified

▪ Use the shortcut **Ctrl+M** to open the Paragraph Specifications dialog box.

▪ Use the shortcut **Ctrl+I** to open the Indents/tabs dialog box.

▪ To turn hyphenation on or off for all text blocks in your document, choose the Pointer tool, open the Hyphenation dialog box and click the **On** or **Off** button.

▪ To turn hyphenation on or off for individual text blocks, click in each text block with the Text tool, then open the Hyphenation dialog box and choose **On** or **Off**. The easiest way to enable hyphenation for certain text blocks is to use styles, explained in Chapter 7.

Quick Work Tips

Dressing Up Text

TYPOGRAPHY CAN ADD MOOD and emotion to your words. Used properly, the right typographic touch, combined with the proper use of space on the page, enhances your documents in subtle, often subliminal ways. PageMaker is well known for its ability to control type and space.

This chapter shows you how to select the font you want, in the right size and style. You will also learn how to present that font in the space it needs to be read and understood. PageMaker's leading, kerning and tracking controls make adding the right amount of space easy.

The classic definition of a font is all the characters of a specific typeface. For the purposes of this book, you can think of the terms *font* and *typeface* interchangeably. For programs like PageMaker, fonts are specifically named faces that are stored in your computer and download to the printer as a part of your print job.

Introduction

Accessing Your Fonts

Whether you have installed PostScript Type-1 fonts or TrueType fonts, they will work equally well with PageMaker and your laser printer—be it a PostScript printer or a PCL printer (like a Hewlett-Packard). Just remember that for your PostScript fonts to operate correctly, they must be copied to your PC's PSFonts folder **(Figure 1)**. PageMaker offers several ways to select a default font:

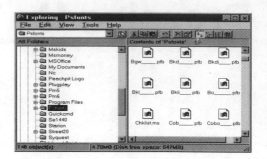

Figure 1 *Only PostScript fonts copied to the PSFonts folder are available for PageMaker.*

■ To choose a default font for a specific document, open the document, click the Pointer tool and select the font. Now each time you choose the Text tool, click open a text block and begin typing, the text will be in the default font you se- lected. To choose a different font, click the Text tool in the text block, then se- lect the font.

■ To choose a default font for all new documents, start PageMaker, but don't open a document, or create a new docu- ment. With just the menu bar displayed, click open the type menu and select a font from the Font submenu.

■ To change fonts for text already typed, choose the Text tool, highlight the text you want to change and pick a new font.

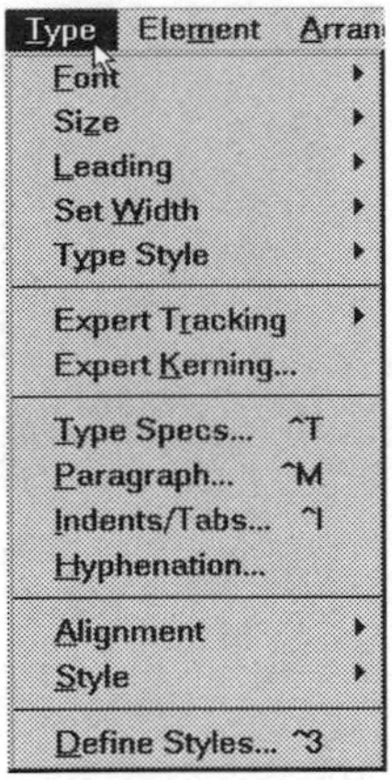

Type	Element	Arran
Font	▸
Size	▸
Leading	▸
Set Width	▸
Type Style	▸

| Expert Tracking | ▸ |
| Expert Kerning... |

Type Specs...	^T
Paragraph...	^M
Indents/Tabs...	^I
Hyphenation...

| Alignment | ▸ |
| Style | ▸ |

| Define Styles... | ^3 |

Figure 2 *Choose the Font command on the Type menu.*

More	▸
Abadi MT Condensed Light
AG Old Face Outline
AGaramond
AGaramond Bold
Anna
Arial
Arial Black
Arial Narrow
AvantGarde
Barmeno ExtraBold
Baskerville BE Regular
Bellevue
Benguiat
Berthold Script Regular
Biffo MT
Blackoak
Bodoni PosterCompressed
Bookman
Boton Regular
Boulevard
Carta
Castellar MT
City Medium
Colossalis Bold
Comic Sans MS
Copperplate Gothic Bold
Copperplate Gothic Light

Figure 3 *Choose the font you want from the menu, or click the arrow to see more fonts.*

Choosing Fonts from the Menu

To select a font for a newly created text block:

1 Click the Text tool where you want the text block, then click open the Type menu and choose the Font command **(Figure 2)**.

2 PageMaker will open the Font submenu **(Figure 3)**, displaying the fonts installed in your system. If you have more fonts than PageMaker can show, click the down arrow to scroll down the menu, or the up arrow to move up.

3 Click the font you want. PageMaker will add a check mark to the font name and return to your document.

Specifying Fonts

Choosing Fonts from the Type Specifications Dialog Box

PageMaker collects several of the font-oriented commands on the Type menu and combines them into one dialog box, called the Type Specifications dialog box. It is handy to use if only because it saves time over choosing the individual commands on the Type menu.

1 Click open the Type menu, and choose the **Type Specs** command **(Figure 4)**.

2 PageMaker will open the Type Specifications dialog box **(Figure 5)**.

3 Click open the **Font** list box **(Figure 6)**, and choose the font you want.

4 Click OK to return to your document.

Tip

An easy shortcut to remember for the Type Specifications dialog box is **Ctrl+T**.

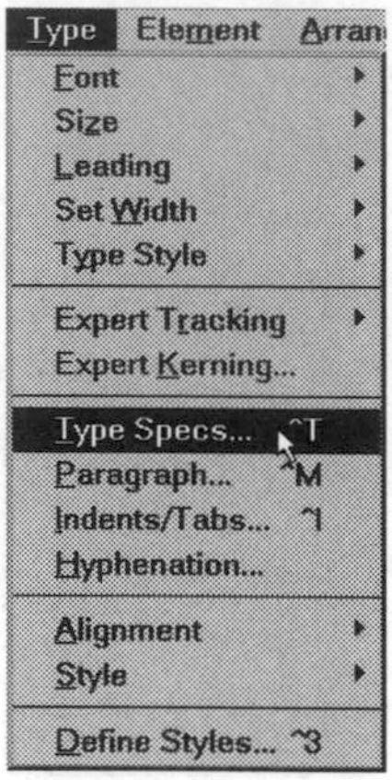

Figure 4 *Choose the Type Specs command on the Type menu.*

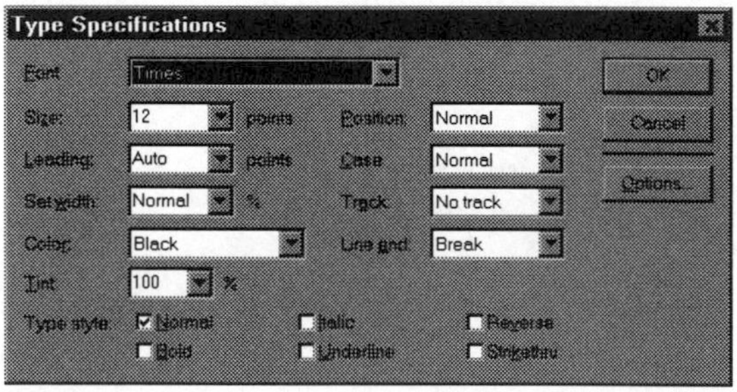

Figure 5 *Type Specifications dialog box.*

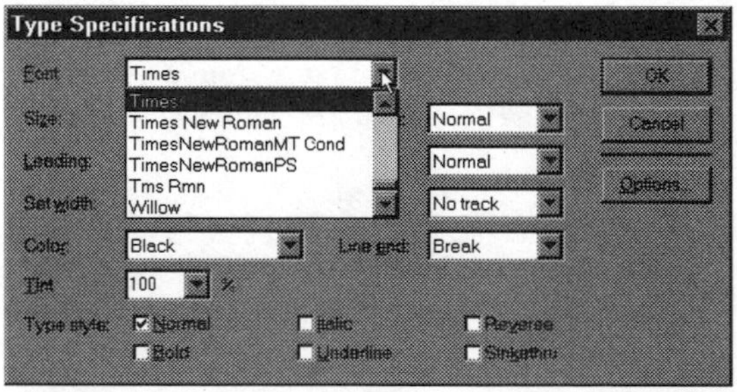

Figure 6 *Click the Font list box to pop open the font menu.*

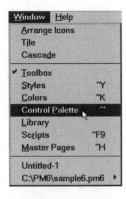

Figure 7 *Choose the Control Palette command on the Window menu.*

Choosing Fonts from the Control Palette

The Control palette is even faster to use than the Type Specifications dialog box because you can experiment with different fonts, and see the results interactively on your document page.

1 Open the Control palette by clicking the Window command and choosing the Control Palette command **(Figure 7)**.

2 Click the Text tool and click on the page where you want to begin typing. (If you want to change text you've already typed, highlight the text with the Text tool.)

3 Notice that when you choose the Text tool, the Control palette changes to the character view **(Figure 8)**. The settings you see in the palette at this point are the default settings for the text you will type.

4 To select a different font, click open the font menu and choose the font you want.

5 To see what different fonts would look like on the page, simply highlight the text you want to experiment with, and choose a font from the palette. The text will be re-displayed with each selection you make.

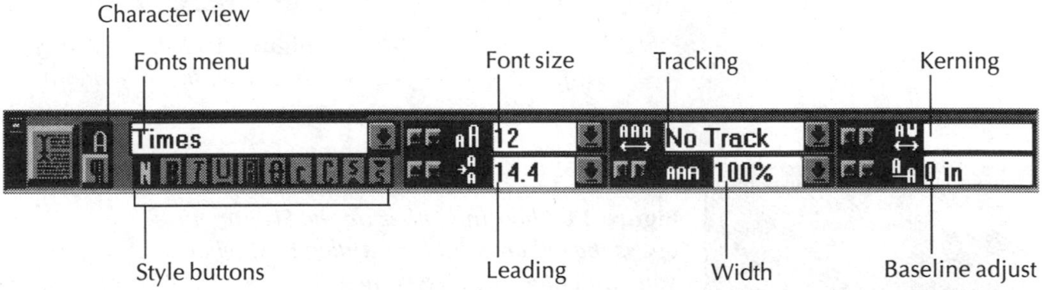

Specifying Fonts

Character view

Fonts menu   Font size   Tracking   Kerning

| | Times | 12 | No Track | |
| | | 14.4 | 100% | 0 in |

Style buttons   Leading   Width   Baseline adjust

Figure 8 *The Control palette character view when you click text tool in a text block.*

Setting Type Size from the Menu

<u>**1**</u> To select a font size for a newly created text block, click the Text tool where you want the text block, then click open the Type menu and choose the Size command **(Figure 9)**.

2 PageMaker will open the Size submenu **(Figure 10)**, displaying preset sizes from 6 to 72 points.

<u>**3**</u> Click the size you want. PageMaker will add a check mark to the size and return to your document.

<u>**4**</u> If you want to select a size not shown in the submenu, choose Other to open the Other Point Size dialog box **(Figure 11)**. Enter the size you want in the text box and choose OK.

Tip

■ You can enter any size type from 4 points to 650 points.

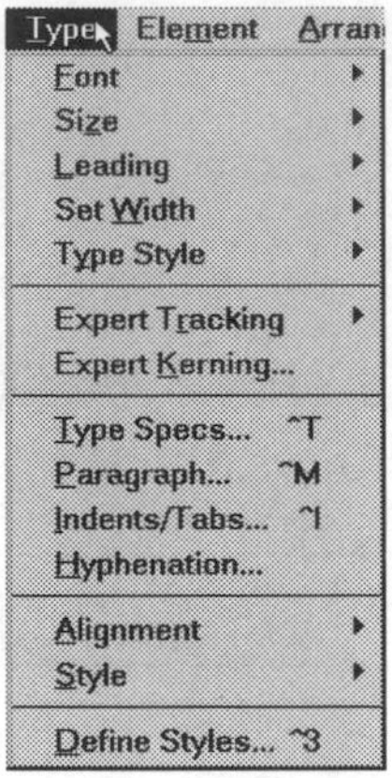

Specifying Type Size

Figure 9 *Choose the Size command on the Type menu.*

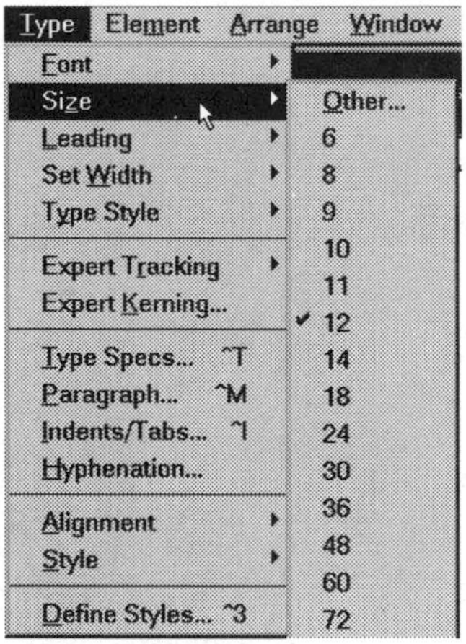

Figure 10 *Select a preset size from the Size menu.*

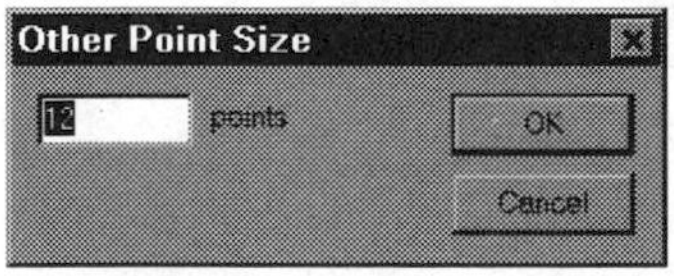

Figure 11 *Choosing Other on the Size menu opens the Other Point Size dialog box, where you can enter any size value.*

Type	Element	Arran:
Font	►	
Size	►	
Leading	►	
Set Width	►	
Type Style	►	
Expert Tracking	►	
Expert Kerning...		
Type Specs...	^T	
Paragraph...	^M	
Indents/Tabs...	^I	
Hyphenation...		
Alignment	►	
Style	►	
Define Styles...	^3	

Figure 12 *Choose the Type Specs command on the Type menu.*

Setting Type Size from the Type Specifications Dialog Box

As with selecting a font, using the Type specifications dialog box to size type is a convenient step-saver.

1 Click open the Type menu, and choose the **Type Specs** command **(Figure 12)**.

2 PageMaker will open the Type Specifications dialog box **(Figure 13)**.

3 Click open the **Size** list box **(Figure 14)**, and choose the font you want, or click in the list box and type the size.

4 Click OK to return to your document.

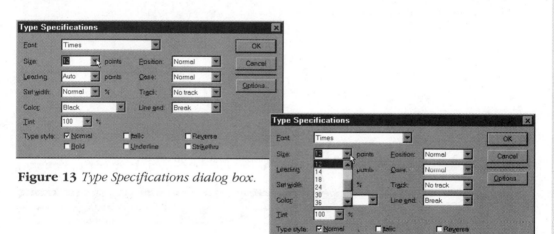

Figure 13 *Type Specifications dialog box.*

Figure 14 *Click the Size list box to pop open the size menu.*

Setting Type Size from the Control Palette

Setting the size of type is just as simple with the Control palette **(Figure 15)**:

1 Simply click the Text tool and

2 Use the size nudge buttons to gradually increase or decrease the size.

3 Or, enter the exact size you want in the size text box.

4 Or, click the size list box arrow to pop open the size menu, and choose the size you want on the menu.

5 To see your text in different sizes, highlight the text first, then open the size menu and try different sizes. Your text will change to reflect your choices.

Size nudge buttons   Size text box   Size list box arrow

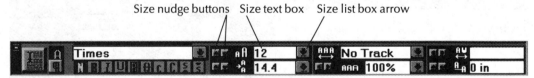

Figure 15 *Control palette character view gives you three different, quick ways to set the size of type.*

Specifying Type Size

Figure 16 *Type style check boxes in the Type Specifications dialog box.*

Type styles

Type styles

Type styles

Type styles

Type styles

~~Type styles~~

About Type Styles

For most fonts, PageMaker offers a choice of eight type styles **(Figure 16)**. You can choose individual styles or combine them for a unique look.

- **Normal**—renders the "normal" appearance—if it is a light version of a font, such as Garamond Light, then the normal style is light; if it is a bold version, such as Helvetica Black, its normal rendering is bold.

- **Bold**—usually a darker, thicker version of the normal style (bold versions of fonts, such as Helvetica Black don't get any bolder when the bold style is added).

- **Italic**—slants the font to the right or gives the font a script appearance.

- **Underline**—adds an underline to characters.

- **Reverse**—changes the characters to white, instead of black.

- **Strikethru**—adds a horizontal line through the middle of the characters.

Tip

- To see reversed type, add a dark colored object behind the type. To "find" reversed type on the white page, choose **Select All** from the Edit menu (or press **Ctrl+A**), then click the text block containing the type.

About Type Styles

Choosing a Type Style from the Menu

To add a type style to the font you have selected:

1 Highlight the text you want to modify, click open the Type menu and choose the Type style command **(Figure 17)**.

2 PageMaker will open the Type style submenu **(Figure 18)**. Choose the style you want (the styles you select will display check marks when you open the menu again).

Tip

▪ While you can assign as many styles to type as you wish, doing so may create some unattractive results. It is wise to be frugal when applying more than one style to type.

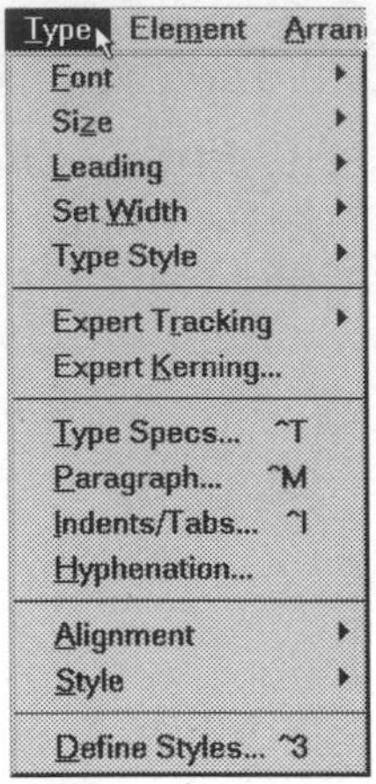

Figure 17 *Choose the Type Style command on the Type menu.*

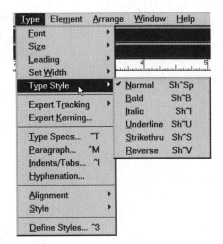

Figure 18 *Check mark on the Type Style submenu shows which style is currently in effect.*

Specifying Type Styles

Choosing a Type Style from the Type Specifications Dialog Box

1 Choose the Text tool and highlight the text you want to add a type style to.

2 Choose the Type Specs command on the Type menu to open the Type Specifications dialog box **(Figure 19)**.

3 In the Type style area, click the appropriate check boxes to add the styles to your text **(Figure 20)**.

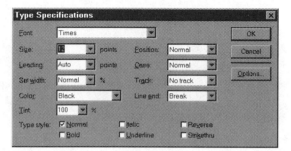

Figure 19 *Type Specifications dialog box.*

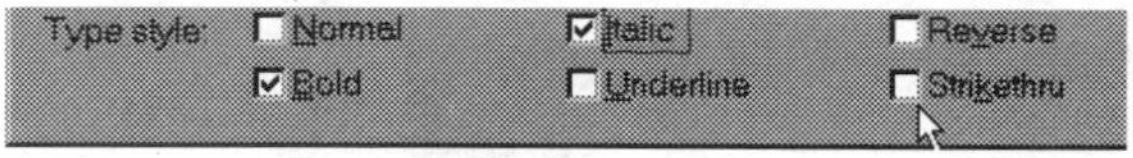

Figure 20 *Click the style check boxes you want to assign to type.*

Specifying Type Styles

Choosing a Type Style from the Control Palette

1 Choose the Text tool and highlight the text you want to add a type style to.

2 Choose the style or styles you want from the palette **(Figure 21)**.

3 Click the style button you want to apply the style to the text you have highlighted. The button will blacken, indicating it is activated.

4 To remove the style, click the button a second time. To remove all styles, click the Normal button.

Specifying Type Styles

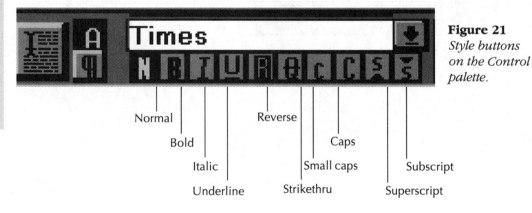

Figure 21
Style buttons on the Control palette.

Normal

Bold

Italic

Underline

Reverse

Strikethru

Caps

Small caps

Superscript

Subscript

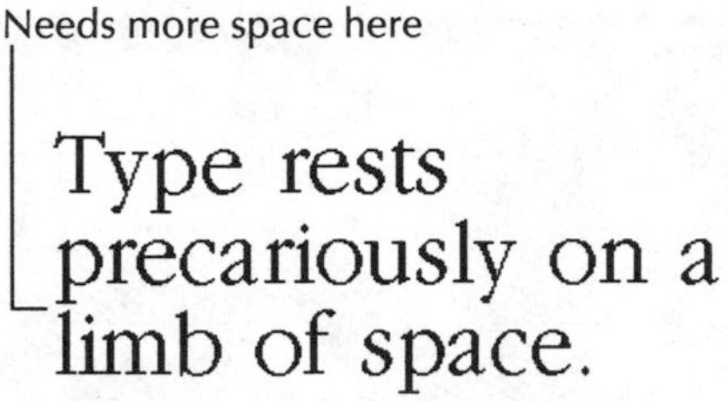

Needs more space here

Type rests
precariously on a
limb of space.

Figure 22 *Lack of space between lines makes the type appear unbalanced and awkward.*

Needs kerning here

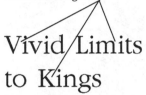

Vivid Limits
to Kings

Figure 23 *Some pairs of letters, often with i as one of the letters, have too much space and require kerning.*

Understanding Space

In typography, space is as important as type. Space gives type room to breathe, room to help readers absorb the text, and room to provide contrast between the black of the type and the white of the page. There are several kinds of space involved in dressing up your type:

- **Leading**—is the space between lines of type. Leading size includes the type size, plus some extra to provide the space between lines. So if you set the type at 10 points and specified 10 points of leading, the bottom of the descenders of one line would butt against the top of the ascenders of the next line **(Figure 22)**. Generally, leading should be about 120 percent of the type size (12 points of leading for 10 point type).

- **Letter space**—is the amount of space between the letters of a word. PageMaker lets you define the minimum and maximum amount of letter space for a paragraph. Letter space limits are set in the Paragraph specifications dialog box.

- **Word space**—is the space created when you press the Spacebar. Yet PageMaker allows minimum and maximum word space limits. Word space is adjusted in the Paragraph Specifications dialog box.

- **Kerning**—is the act of removing letter space from pairs of letters. Some combinations of letters just seem spaced too far apart **(Figure 23)**. PageMaker can automatically kern certain pairs of letters. You can also manually kern those pairs or any letter pair.

- **Tracking**—is the same as kerning only for more than a pair of letters. Normally, you adjust tracking for words, sentences or paragraphs.

About Space

Changing Letter Space and Word Space

1 Select the Text tool in the toolbox and click anywhere in the text block whose letter space you want to change.

2 Open the Type menu and choose the Paragraph command (or press **Ctrl+M**) to open the Paragraph Specifications dialog box **(Figure 24)**.

3 Click **Spacing** to open the Paragraph Spacing Attributes dialog box **(Figure 25)**.

4 Change the Minimum, Desired, and Maximum values for word space and letter space to suit your document. The Desired value is the spacing recommended by the font's designer. Minimum and Maximum values are how tight and how loose PageMaker is allowed to make the spacing.

5 To reduce spacing, make the minimum and maximum values closer to 100. To increase spacing, enter a broader range for the two values.

6 Hold down the Control button and click OK to save the new values and return directly to your document.

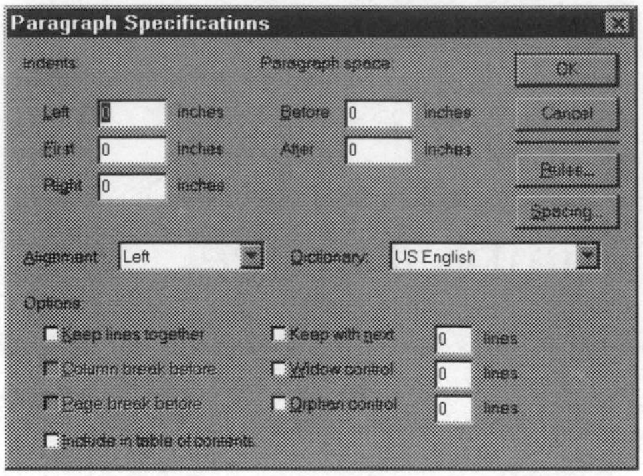

Figure 24 *Paragraph Specifications dialog box.*

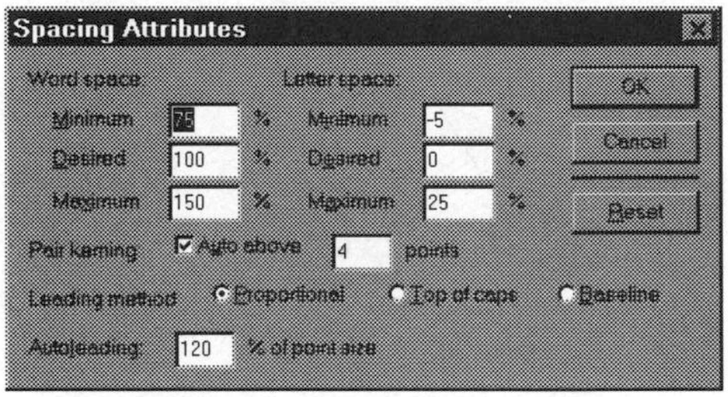

Figure 25 *Paragraph Spacing Attributes dialog box controls the minimum and maximum spacing between letters and words.*

Setting Letter and Word Space

Enter the point size at which you want
kerning here

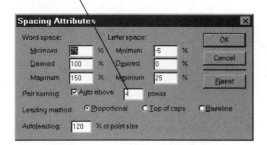

Figure 26 *Control when type is
automatically kerned by setting a
minimum size in the Paragraph
Spacing Attributes dialog box.*

Adjusting Automatic Kerning

Normally, PageMaker is configured to
automatically kern certain letter pair combinations above 4 points (meaning kerning is
done for all sizes of type). Yet kerning is
most effective (and the need for kerning
most obvious) in larger type sizes. To adjust
the minimum size at which PageMaker begins kerning:

1 Click open the Type menu and choose
Paragraph (or press **Ctrl+M**) to open the
Paragraph Specifications dialog box.

2 Click the **Spacing** button to open the
Paragraphs Spacing Attributes dialog
box **(Figure 26)**.

3 In the Pair kerning area, enter the minimum size to kern type (try starting with
24 points).

4 To turn automatic kerning off, click the
Auto check box to remove the X.

How to Manually Kern Letter Pairs

While PageMaker's auto kerning is fine for many instances, sometimes you may want to manually change the space between letters. Here's how:

1 Click the Text tool from the toolbox and click the insertion point between the two letters you want to adjust.

2 Choose a magnified view of the two letters—press **Ctrl+2** to increase the view to 200%.

3 Use the keyboard shortcuts in the table below to increase or decrease space between letters.

Tip

▪ To undo any manual kerning applied to characters, position the insertion point between the kerned letters and press **Shift+Ctrl+0**.

Kerning Pairs of Letters

To kern by this amount	Use this key combination
Increase space in 1/25th em	Ctrl++ (Plus on keypad)
Decrease space in 1/25th em	Ctrl+- (Minus on keypad)
Increase space in 1/100th em	Ctrl+Shift++ (Plus on keypad)
Decrease space in 1/100th em	Ctrl+Shift+- (Minus on keypad)

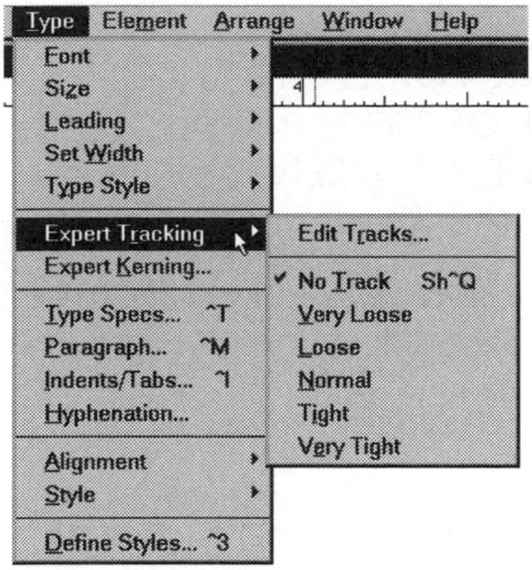

Type	Element	Arrange	Window	Help
Font ▸				
Size ▸				
Leading ▸				
Set Width ▸				
Type Style ▸				
Expert Tracking ▸	Edit Tracks...			
Expert Kerning...	✓ No Track Sh^Q			
Type Specs... ^T	Very Loose			
Paragraph... ^M	Loose			
Indents/Tabs... ¬	Normal			
Hyphenation...	Tight			
Alignment ▸	Very Tight			
Style ▸				
Define Styles... ^3				

Figure 27 *Choose the Expert Tracking command on the Type menu to open the tracking submenu.*

Adjusting Tracking

PageMaker offers six levels of tracking control, starting with no tracking at all and moving from very loose to very tight.

1   Highlight the text you want to modify.

2   Open the Type menu and choose the Expert Tracking command.

3   In the Expert Tracking submenu **(Figure 27)**, select the amount of tracking you want to apply to the selected text. Examples of tracking are shown in **Figure 28**.

Expert tracking—— No tracking

Expert tracking—— Very loose

Expert tracking—— Loose

Expert tracking—— Normal

Expert tracking—— Tight

Expert tracking—— Very tight

Figure 28 *Examples of PageMaker's track settings.*

Specifying Tracking

Changing Leading from the Menu

Before computers replaced typewriters, we used to add more space between lines of typing by setting the line spacing switch at 2 or 3, meaning we'd add two or three blank lines between each typed line. While some word processors still deal with line spacing that way, PageMaker adds leading to the line to create the space between lines of type **(Figure 29)**. While the default setting is 120 percent of the type size, you can change leading at any time.

1   Choose the Text tool and highlight the text you want to modify.

2   Open the Type menu and choose the Leading command.

3   In the Leading submenu **(Figure 30)**, choose the amount of leading you want.

4   Choose **Auto** to let PageMaker determine the leading, based on the size of the type.

5   Notice that most of the leading sizes are close to the type size. If you want an unusually large or small amount of leading, choose **Other** to open the Other Leading dialog box **(Figure 31)**. Enter the exact amount of leading in the text box.

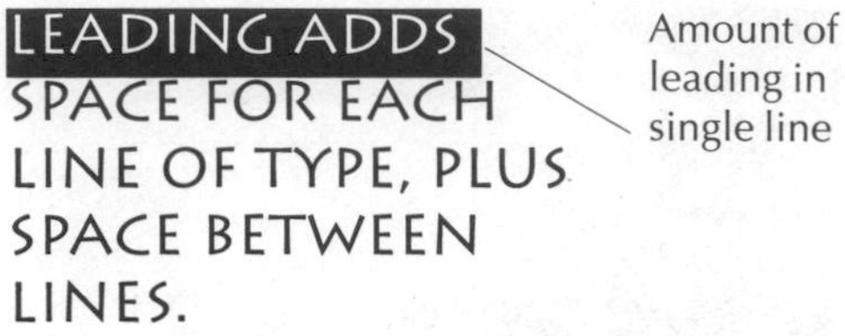

LEADING ADDS SPACE FOR EACH LINE OF TYPE, PLUS SPACE BETWEEN LINES.

Amount of leading in single line

Figure 29 *Leading shown in black slug for a line of type.*

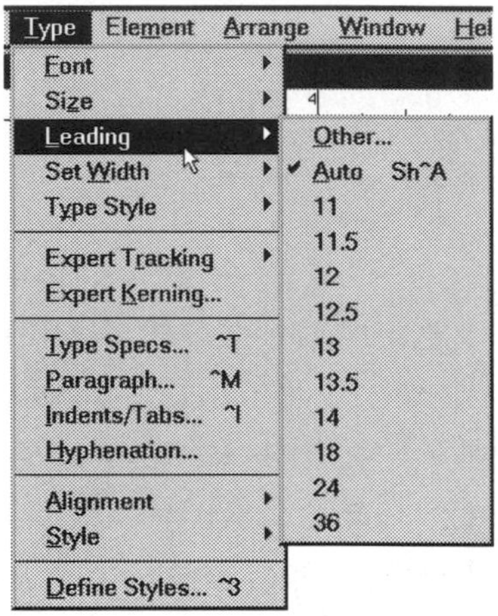

Figure 30 *Choose the Leading command on the Type menu to open the leading submenu.*

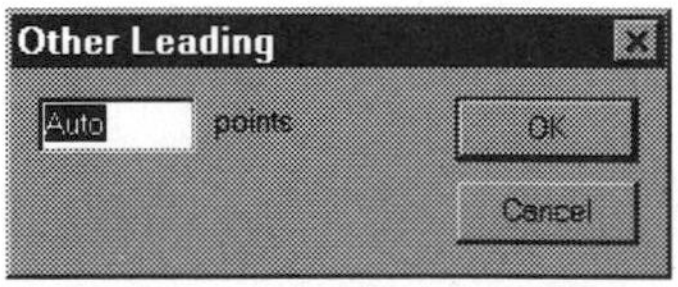

Figure 31 *Other Leading dialog box lets you enter any leading value in up to tenths of a point.*

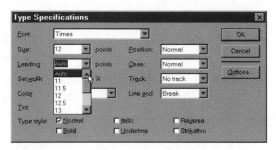

Figure 32 *Type the leading value in the Leading text box, or click the box arrow and choose a value from the menu.*

Changing Leading from the Type Specifications Dialog Box

1 Choose the Text tool and highlight the text you want to add a type style to.

2 Open the Type menu and choose the Type Specs command.

3 In the Type Specifications dialog box **(Figure 32)**, enter the amount of leading you want in the Leading text box.

Changing Leading from the Control Palette

1 Choose the Text tool and highlight the text you want to add a type style to.

2 Open the Control palette by clicking the Window menu and choose the Control Palette command.

3 Click open the leading menu in the Control palette **(Figure 33)** or type the specific amount of leading in the text box.

4 Use the nudge buttons to slowly increment the leading value up or down.

Specifying Leading

Size nudge buttons   Size text box   Size list box arrow

Figure 33 *Control palette character view gives three ways to quickly adjust leading.*

Changing Space Above and Below Paragraphs

Pressing the Return key twice between paragraphs is a crude way to add space between paragraphs, but not the ideal way. PageMaker offers a specific method to have more space between paragraphs than the line leading of paragraph text.

1 Open the Type command and choose the Paragraph command.

2 In the Paragraph Specifications dialog box **(Figure 34)**, enter the amount of additional space you want in either the **Before** or **After** text boxes.

Tip

■ If you enter a value in both the Before and the After boxes, you will effectively double the amount of space between all but the top and bottom paragraphs **(Figure 35)**.

Enter the amount of space **Before** or **After** paragraphs, here

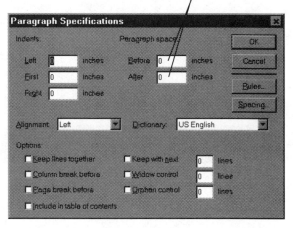

Figure 34 *Paragraph Specifications dialog box controls space above and below paragraphs.*

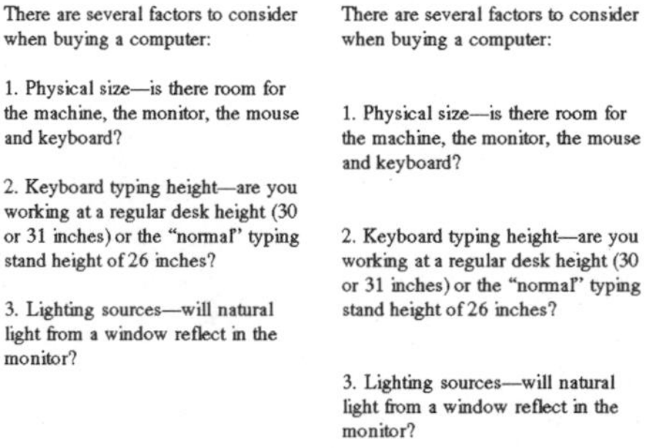

There are several factors to consider when buying a computer:

1. Physical size—is there room for the machine, the monitor, the mouse and keyboard?

2. Keyboard typing height—are you working at a regular desk height (30 or 31 inches) or the "normal" typing stand height of 26 inches?

3. Lighting sources—will natural light from a window reflect in the monitor?

There are several factors to consider when buying a computer:

1. Physical size—is there room for the machine, the monitor, the mouse and keyboard?

2. Keyboard typing height—are you working at a regular desk height (30 or 31 inches) or the "normal" typing stand height of 26 inches?

3. Lighting sources—will natural light from a window reflect in the monitor?

Figure 35 *Examples of setting space before (left) and setting space both before and after paragraphs, which doubles paragraph spacing.*

Space Between Paragraphs

The baseline is an invisible line on which each line of type rests.

Figure 36 *Baselines shown illustrate how lines of type rest on invisible baselines.*

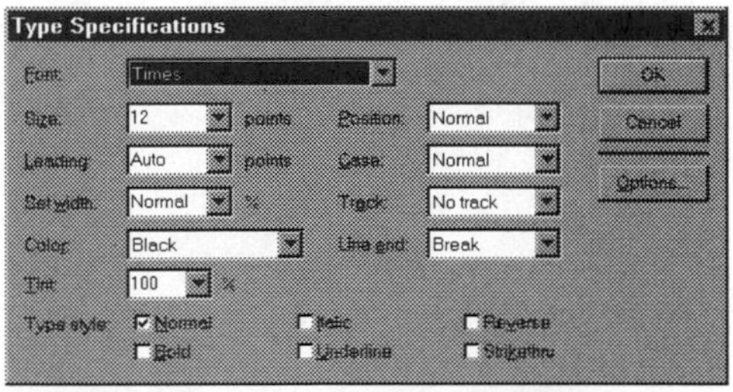

Type Specifications				
Font:	Times			OK
Size:	12 ▼ points	Position:	Normal ▼	Cancel
Leading:	Auto ▼ points	Case:	Normal ▼	Options...
Set width:	Normal ▼ %	Track:	No track ▼	
Color:	Black ▼	Line end:	Break ▼	
Tint:	100 ▼ %			
Type style:	☑ Normal ☐ Bold	☐ Italic ☐ Underline	☐ Reverse ☐ Strikethru	

Figure 37 *To adjust baselines, click the Options button in the Type Specifications dialog box.*

Type Options		
Small caps size:	70 % of point size	OK
Super/subscript size:	58.3 % of point size	Cancel
Superscript position:	33.3 % of point size	
Subscript position:	33.3 % of point size	
Baseline shift:	0 points ⦿ Up ○ Down	

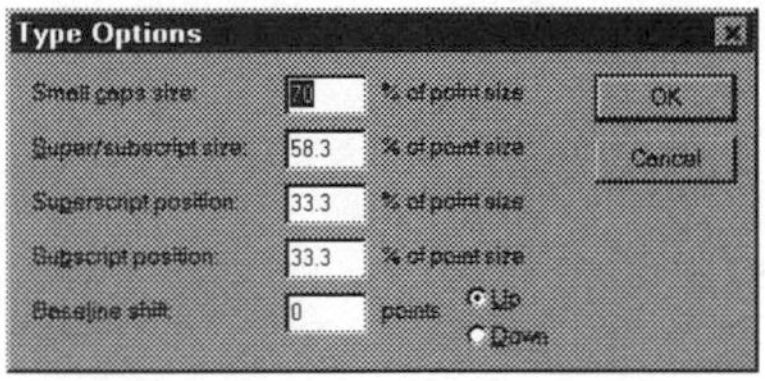

Figure 38 *Use the Type Options dialog box to enter the amount of baseline shift (in points) and the direction.*

Shifting Type Up or Down

All the characters that you type in PageMaker rest on an invisible line, called the *baseline* **(Figure 36)**. When characters are subscripted or superscripted, the baseline for those characters is simply shifted down or up, respectively. To control the amount of shift, follow these steps:

1 Choose the Text tool and highlight the characters whose baseline you want to shift.

2 Click open the Type menu and choose the Type Specs command.

3 In the Type Specifications dialog box **(Figure 37)**, click the **Options** button to open the Type Options dialog box **(Figure 38)**.

4 Enter the amount of shift in the Baseline shift text box and click the **Up** or **Down** button to indicate the direction of baseline shift. The shifted baseline might look something like **Figure 39** which is raised 6 points.

The baseline is an ^{invisible} line on which each line of type rests.

Figure 39 *Example of a raised baseline.*

Quick and Easy Work Habits

▪ For many of the type formatting options there are three ways to access them in PageMaker: from the Type menu, using the Type Specifications dialog box, or by using the Control palette. While I've shown you how to use all three ways, the palette is by far the easiest and quickest.

▪ And, as I've pointed out, using the palette lets you see interactive changes to your work: Highlight the text, pick a new format on the palette and the highlighted text will assume that format. Don't like it? Without re-highlighting, just pick the original format or try something different. It's easy to fiddle with the Control palette, and keeps you from having to jump back and forth from your text to a menu or dialog box.

▪ I tend to depend on the palette for most formatting. A quick **Ctrl+T** will jump you to the Type specifications dialog box for more concentrated formatting. I stopped using the formatting submenus on the Type menu after about the first week of using PageMaker (more than 10 years ago).

Managing Files

HERE IS HOUSEKEEPING HELP to keep your documents under control—from how to save your work, to how to copy documents to floppies and removable drives. Basic stuff, but unbelievably important when the lights suddenly go off, your computer winds down, and you sit there in disbelief.

I strongly suggest that you save your documents often. There's no better advice when working in PageMaker. PageMaker has no automatic save feature, and if you suffer even the briefest of power failures—even a mere dimming of the lights—you will likely lose anything you added to your document since the last time you saved your work. PageMaker, in fact, has some means of recovering after a power failure, which you will learn about in this chapter.

Introduction

Saving Your New Document

One of the things that PageMaker should be able to do, but can't, is automatically save your work. Since PageMaker still makes you save manually, you should do so regularly and often. Saving a new document for the first time forces you to name the document and assign it to a particular folder in your computer. Once that is done, saving is less intrusive; just choose the Save command on the File menu (or use the easy shortcut **Ctrl+S**) and PageMaker quickly saves your work. To save a new document:

1 Click open the File menu and choose the Save command **(Figure 1)**.

2 PageMaker will open the Save publication as dialog box **(Figure 2)**.

3 Type a document name in the file name text box.

4 Then, decide where you want to store the document.

5 Click OK to return to your document.

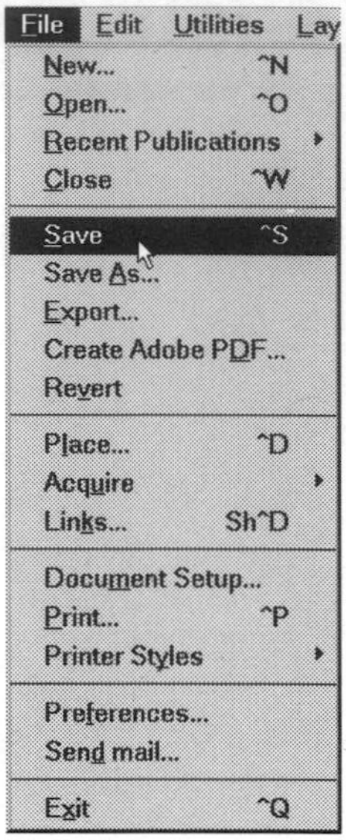

Tips

▌ It's best not to save your documents to PageMaker's default directory where all of its programs are located. Instead, create work-related, or client-related folders and save your jobs there.

▌ Remember to save often. How often? Just keep in mind that you risk losing whatever hasn't been saved, so if you can afford to recreate an hour's work, you need only save once an hour. I save about every five minutes—**Ctrl+S** is all it takes.

Figure 1 *Choose the Save command on the File menu.*

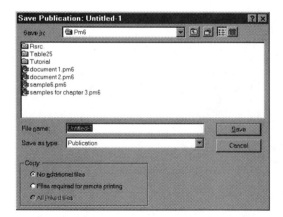

Figure 2 *Use the Save publication as dialog box to name your new document.*

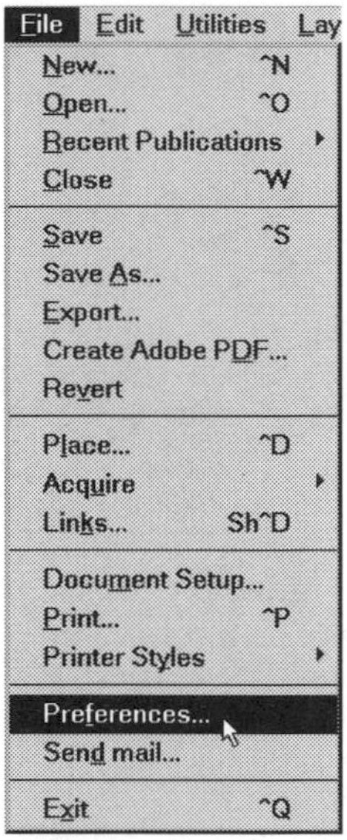

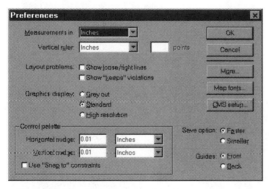

Figure 3 *Choose the Preferences command on the File menu.*

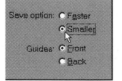

Figure 4 *Preferences dialog box controls how fast PageMaker saves documents.*

Figure 5 *Click Save Smaller option to control file size.*

Saving Faster Vs. Saving Smaller

PageMaker files can get pretty large—their size can reach megabyte proportions, in fact. It's tempting to ask PageMaker to save as fast as possible. Yet doing so only makes the file sizes increase. You see, PageMaker keeps track of just about everything you do, including the last-saved version of your document, fonts added and later deleted, even graphics added and later removed. It even saves the parts of your documents that take up too much memory. Sometimes, even when you delete a lot of pages, your document will still grow each time it's saved.

To rein in the size of your files, choose the save smaller option in the Preferences dialog box. When Save smaller is selected instead of the default Save faster setting, your documents might take a moment longer to be saved, but they will be considerably smaller. To choose the option:

1 Click open the File menu and choose the Preferences command **(Figure 3)**.

2 In the Preferences dialog box **(Figure 4)**, click the Smaller radio button **(Figure 5)** if it isn't already selected.

3 Click OK to save the preference and return to your document.

Tip

▦ Another way to reduce the size of your document is to use PageMaker's Save As command, on the File menu. Choose it and save the document with a different name.

Saving Smaller Files

Undoing What You Just Did

When you find you're talking to yourself, muttering, "Why did I just do that?" keep in mind PageMaker has an Undo command which will undo the most recent thing that you've done. It will, for instance, save your skin when you delete text you just wrote. It will undo a graphic that you accidentally moved. And, it will reposition an element that you didn't mean to resize. The key to the Undo command is that it can only act on the most immediate event. If you delete something and then type some text, the undo command will undo the typing but it won't be able to undelete the text. To undo your last action:

1 Click open the Edit menu and find the Undo command **(Figure 6)**. The command will indicate what it is capable of undoing (if a delete occurred it will say Undo Delete, if you just typed some text the command will say Undo Edit, etc.).

2 Click the command to undo the last thing you did.

Tips

■ An easy shortcut to the Undo command is **Ctrl+Z**.

■ The Undo command can even undo itself. Choose the command to undo something. After the action is undone, open the Edit menu again and notice the command. It will be ready to Redo whatever it just undid. For example if you deleted some text, the Undo command would say Undo Delete. If you then clicked the command, the deleted text would reappear on the page and the command would say Redo Delete.

Figure 6 *Choose the Undo command on the Edit menu.*

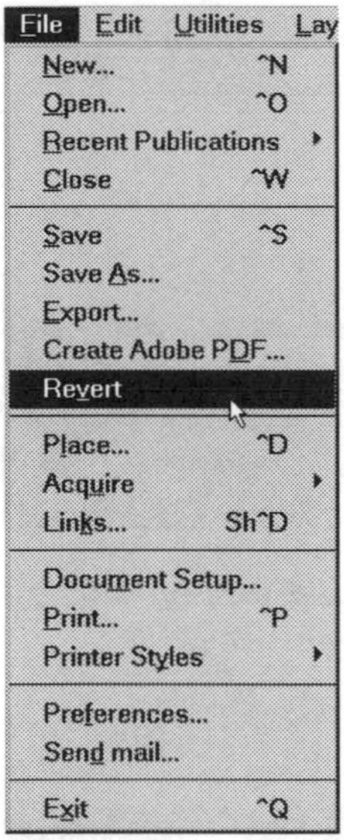

Figure 7 *Choose the Revert command on the File menu.*

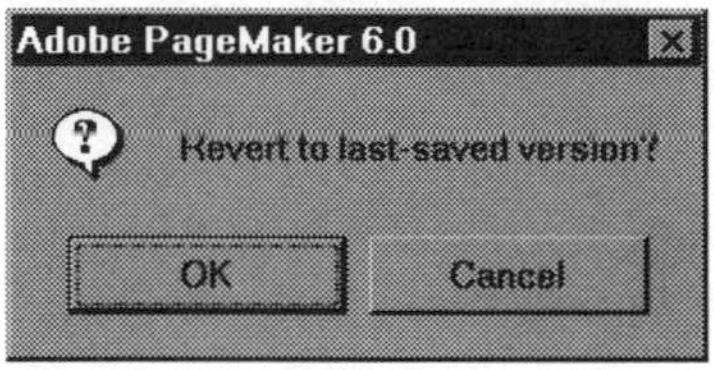

Figure 8 *PageMaker warns you before reverting to a previously saved version of your document.*

Reverting to the Last-Saved Version

When you need to undo something you've done, and you missed the opportunity to use the Undo command, you may still be able to get back to where you were by using PageMaker's Revert command. Revert takes you back to the last saved version of your document. It does the same thing as closing your document without saving it—you will lose anything you have done after the last time you saved the document. To revert:

1 Open the File menu and choose the Revert command **(Figure 7)**. If the command is grayed out, it means you have not yet saved your document for the first time.

2 Choose the command. PageMaker will show you a warning dialog box **(Figure 8)**. Click OK to proceed, choose Cancel to return to your document without reverting.

Tip

▪ Remember, the Revert command is an all-or-nothing deal. If you revert you lose everything you've done since the last time you saved. To minimize the effects of the Revert command, get in the habit of saving often.

Reverting

Recovering From a Power Outage

If your computer isn't connected to an uninterruptable power supply, someday the lights will go blip and your computer will restart. Anything not yet saved will be lost (yet another reason to save often). Normally, you will have to redo whatever work you had done after the last save. To recover a new document not yet saved, follow these steps:

1 Restart PageMaker. Open the File menu and choose the Open command.

2 In the Open Publication dialog box **(Figure 9)**, locate the Temp folder (usually inside the Windows 95 folder) and open it **(Figure 10)**.

3 If PageMaker was able to save a temporary version of the new document, you will see PM6533T.TMP (or a similar number—the T meaning a new temporary file).

4 Open the file and immediately save it as a new document (use the Save command on the File menu or press **Ctrl+S**).

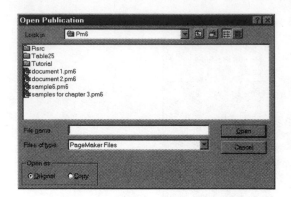

Figure 9 *Use the Open publication dialog box to file PageMaker's temporary files.*

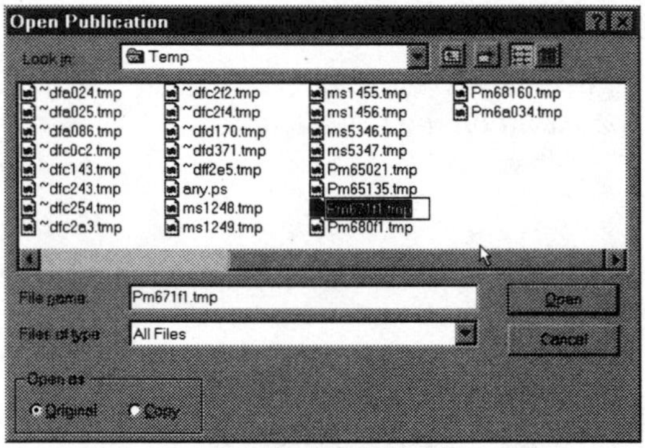

Figure 10 *Temporary files will help you recover from power failures.*

Recovering Files

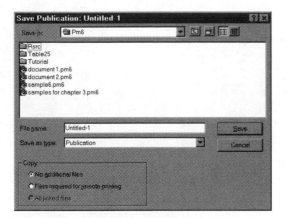

Figure 11 *Copy documents to floppies or removable media with the Save publication as dialog box.*

Copying Files to Floppy Disks

Eventually you will need to copy a document to a floppy disk (or a removable cartridge drive, such as a Bernoulli or Syquest drive). You may have a system at work and a system at home and want to work on your document in both places. Maybe you want to ship a document to another office for review or printing. Whatever the reason, it's easy to copy PageMaker files, using either PageMaker or Explorer. Here are the steps:

1   From PageMaker, open the File menu and choose the Save As command.

2   PageMaker will display the Save publication as dialog box **(Figure 11)**. Choose a floppy disk , or the removable disk in the **Save in** list box.

3   The current name of the document is displayed in the file name text box. Since you are copying to a removable media you needn't change the document name unless you want to.

4   Choose the **Files for remote printing** radio button to ensure that the necessary files are included with your document (this option does not copy fonts used in your document).

To copy files from Explorer, simply click the PageMaker file and drag it to the floppy disk or removable disk icon on the Windows desktop.

Tip

▪ Copying either from PageMaker or Explorer doesn't disturb the original PageMaker document, but makes a second copy to the removable drive.

Copying to Floppies

Cloning Documents

This is really saving one document with a different name using the Save As command, but I think of it as cloning. There's a good reason for cloning—laziness. If you have a perfectly good PageMaker document that can be the basis for a new document, why reinvent the wheel? Just save the document with a different name, open it up and make the appropriate changes. Likewise, if you want to play around with some changes, to protect your work in the original document, create a clone for experimenting. Then if you like the changes you can save them; if not you can throw the clone in the trash.

To Save one document as another:

1 Open the File menu and choose the Save As command.

2 In the Save publication as dialog box **(Figure 12)**, type a different name for the document.

3 Choose a folder to store the cloned document in.

4 Click the **No additional files** radio button since you won't be remotely printing the clone.

5 Click **Open** to save the document and open it. Now experiment away!

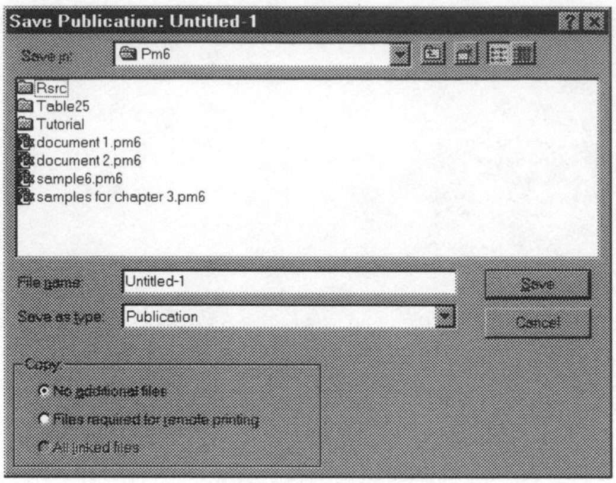

Figure 12 *Use the Save publication as dialog box to save your document with a different name.*

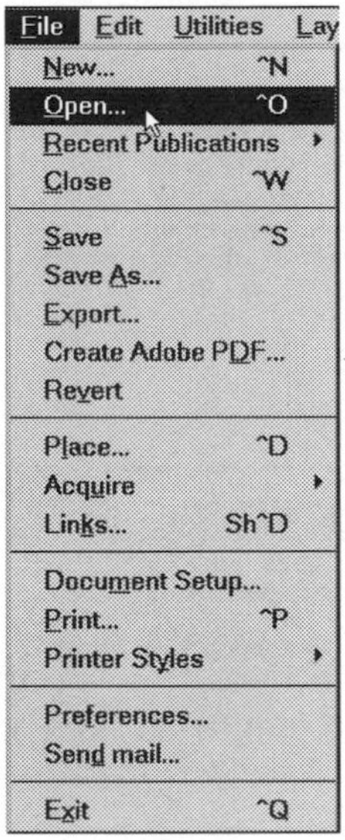

File	Edit	Utilities	Lay
New...			^N
Open...			^O
Recent Publications			▶
Close			^W
Save			^S
Save As...			
Export...			
Create Adobe PDF...			
Revert			
Place...			^D
Acquire			▶
Links...			Sh^D
Document Setup...			
Print...			^P
Printer Styles			▶
Preferences...			
Send mail...			
Exit			^Q

Figure 13 *Choose the Open command on the File menu.*

Opening Copies of Your Documents

I am a great believer in saving time and effort with PageMaker. One of the ways to quickly put together a new document is to base it on something you've already designed. I have explained saving one document as another document—cloning, I call it. You can clone documents using the Save As command, or let PageMaker open a copy of your publications, which you can save with a different name.

1 Click open the File menu and choose the Open command **(Figure 13)**.

2 In the Open publication dialog box **(Figure 14)**, choose the existing PageMaker document you want to open a copy of.

3 Now, click the **Copy** radio button in the Open area (PageMaker defaults to activating the Original button).

4 An unnamed copy of your document will open in PageMaker's layout window. Save it with a new name and use it as the basis for your new document.

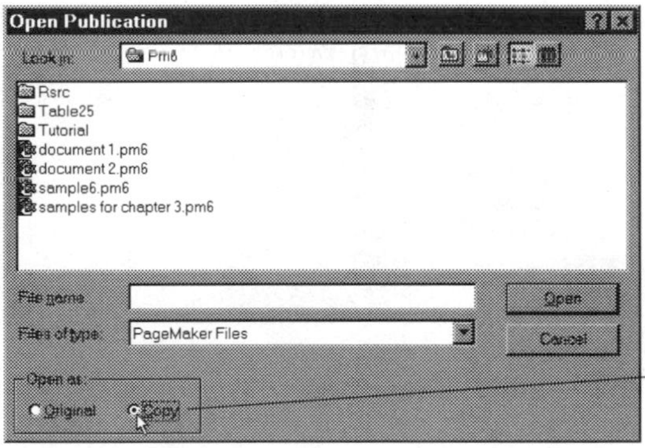

Open Publication

Look in:	Pm6

- Rsrc
- Table25
- Tutorial
- document 1.pm6
- document 2.pm6
- sample6.pm6
- samples for chapter 3.pm6

| File name: | | Open |
| Files of type: | PageMaker Files | Cancel |

Open as:
○ Original ● Copy

Click Copy to open a copy of your document

Figure 14 *The Open publication dialog box can create copies of your documents, preserving the originals.*

Cloning Documents

Renaming Your Documents

It's tempting to use the Save As command to rename your documents. Don't. You will create twice as many documents as you need and it can get confusing. Here's how to change any file name using Explorer:

1 Click the Windows Start button. Choose the Programs folder to open the Programs menu. Then, choose Explorer **(Figure 15)**.

2 Use Explorer to open the folder and find the files you want to rename **(Figure 16)**.

3 Find the file name you want to change. Click to highlight, then click again (not a double-click). The mouse arrow will change to a text insertion point **(Figure 17)**. Type the new name.

4 Click the PageMaker button in the Task bar to return to PageMaker.

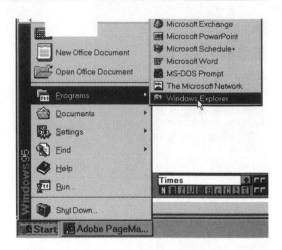

Figure 15 *Click the Start button to open the Program menu and Start Explorer.*

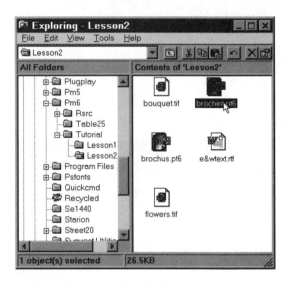

Figure 16 *Open folder in the Explorer.*

Figure 17 *Click the document name, and use the text insertion point to change it.*

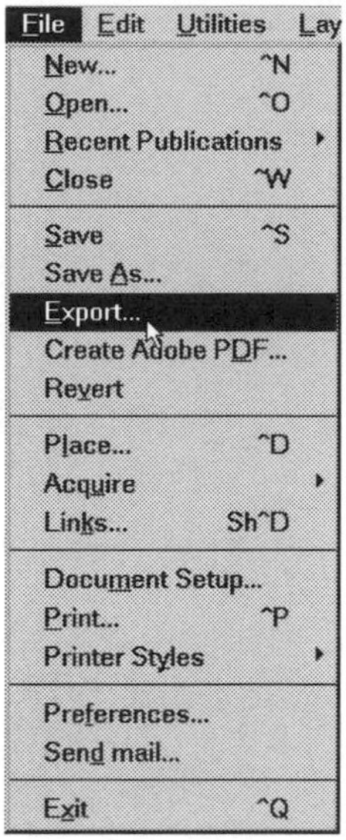

Figure 18 *Choose the Export command on the File menu.*

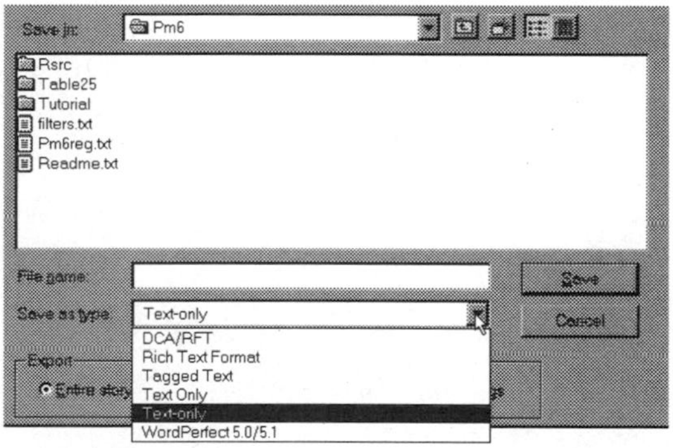

Figure 19 *Use the Export dialog box to export text blocks for use in a word processor.*

Exporting Text

Sometimes it's handy to be able to use text created in PageMaker in a word processor. Exporting text is easy. Here's how:

1 Click the text tool anywhere in the story you want to export.

2 Open the File menu and choose the Export command **(Figure 18)**.

3 PageMaker will display the Export dialog box **(Figure 19)**.

4 First, choose the format for the exported file. You can select from DCA/RFT, Rich Text Format, Tagged Text, Text-Only, or WordPerfect 5.0/5.1 formats.

5 To add formatting tags to the text, click the Export tags check box. The tags allow the story to modified in a word processor and imported back into PageMaker with the formatting intact.

6 Click OK to export the story and return to your document.

Exporting

Quick and Easy Work Habits

■ Save often—I can't stress that enough. Remember that the amount of time you work between saves is the amount of time you will lose and have to replicate if you have a power fluctuation. I have developed the habit of pressing **Ctrl+S** just after I do anything. So, if I type a paragraph of text, I make sure that I press **Ctrl+S**. If I place a graphic, I press **Ctrl+S**. If I modify a header on the master page, I press **Ctrl+S**. It just takes a moment and it saves so much rework.

■ If you are serious about designing in PageMaker, consider adding an uninterruptable power supply to your computer. Then if the power dies you can keep working long enough to save your documents and shut down your computer.

Quick Work Tips

Using Styles

IF YOU ARE WORKING with more than a page or two of text, chances are you will find yourself making repeated changes to format that text exactly right. Headings need just the right touch, which is different for body text. Tables need their own tabs and formatting, bulleted lists need special indents, and so on. Before you know it you can spend all your time changing the formatting of different types of paragraphs throughout your document. Instead, save yourself a lot of trouble and assign each different type of paragraph to a separate style.

PageMaker styles format paragraphs for you. And, with styles you only format the style itself; the style takes care of reformatting all the paragraphs assigned to it. So, instead of making change after change to the different levels of headings, subheadings and paragraphs of text in a multiple-page document, just change the style. And, when you decide Gill Sans Condensed is really the perfect font for your document's body copy, just specify that font in the Body Copy style instead of changing all those paragraphs of text. PageMaker styles guarantee consistency and make it easy to play "what if?" with the design and typography.

Introduction

About the Styles Palette

You assign a paragraph a particular style by one of two ways:

Either choose the Text tool in the toolbox, choose a style and begin typing. Or, if text has already been added, click the Text tool insertion point in the paragraph and choose the style you want.

While you can open the Type menu, choose the Style command and select the style from a submenu, it's a lot easier to use the Styles palette **(Figure 1)**. Open the palette by choosing the Window menu and choose the Styles command. Like all PageMaker palettes it floats, so you can click its title bar and drag it wherever it is most convenient. In the palette you will see the names of all currently defined styles, plus the option No Style.

When the Styles palette is open, it displays the currently assigned style wherever you click the text insertion point. You can change the style of the paragraph just as easily by simply clicking a different style name.

Figure 1 *Styles palette lets you quickly assign styles to paragraphs of text.*

Style Palette

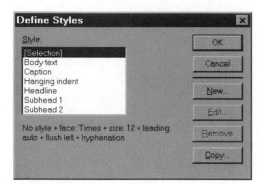

Figure 2 *Define Styles dialog box showing current styles.*

Defining New Styles

PageMaker comes with six predefined styles, shown in the Styles palette. They are a good first step in creating a set of master styles for your documents, but they can definitely be added to and improved. Let's define a new style to add to the list:

1 Click open the Type menu and choose the Define Styles command to open the Define Styles dialog box **(Figure 2)**.

2 Click the **New** button to open the Edit Style dialog box **(Figure 3)**.

3 Type a name for the style in the Name text box. If you want to base this style on an existing style click the style name in the Based on list box. Similarly, if you want to specify which style follows this style (such as the body text style always following the headline style) choose the style that follows in the Next style list box.

4 Now click the appropriate buttons to make style settings for type, paragraphs, tabs and hyphenation.

Enter the name for the style here

Base the new style on an existing style and you save configuring it again

Choose the style you want to assign to the very next paragraph

Shows the current specifications for the style

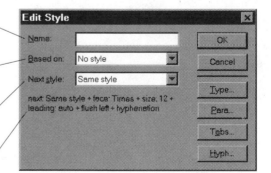

Figure 3 *Edit Style dialog box configures new styles and modifies existing styles.*

Adding Type Characteristics

1 To add type characteristics, press the **Type** button. PageMaker will open the Type Specifications dialog box **(Figure 4)**.

2 Make whatever choices you want to se-lect the font, leading, and type styles for this style. If you have based this style on an existing style, that style's type speci-fications will be shown in the dialog box.

3 Click OK to return to the Edit Style dia-log box.

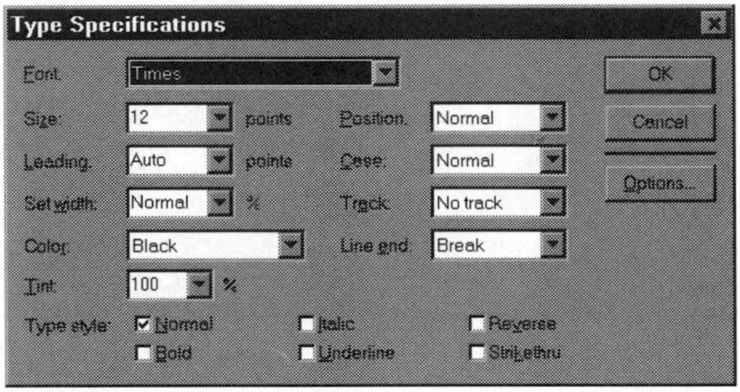

Figure 4 *Type Specifications dialog box configures typographic requirements for the style.*

Adding Paragraph Characteristics

1 If you want to add paragraph characteristics, click the **Para** button to open the Paragraph Specifications dialog box **(Figure 5)**.

2 Make whatever changes you want to the dialog box.

3 Click the **Rules** button to add lines above or below paragraphs in this style.

4 Click the **Spacing** button to increase or decrease the amount of letter and word space for text in this style.

5 Click OK to return to the Edit Style dialog box.

Tip

◼ If this style is for a heading and the document will eventually have a table of contents, click the **Include in table of contents** check box to add an X. (See Chapter 13 for more information about tables of contents.)

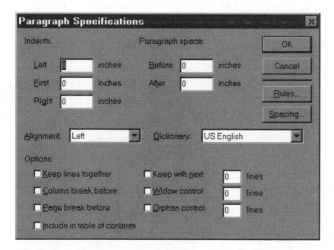

Figure 5 *Add paragraph settings to your styles with the Paragraph Specifications dialog box.*

Adding Tab Characteristics

1 If you want to set tab stops for text in this style, click the **Tabs** button to open the Indents/Tabs dialog box **(Figure 6)**.

2 Choose whatever tab and indent settings you want for text in this style.

3 Click OK to return to the Edit Style dialog box.

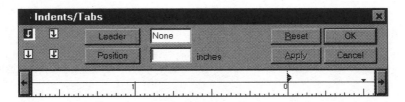

Figure 6 *Make specific tabs settings using the Indents/Tabs dialog box.*

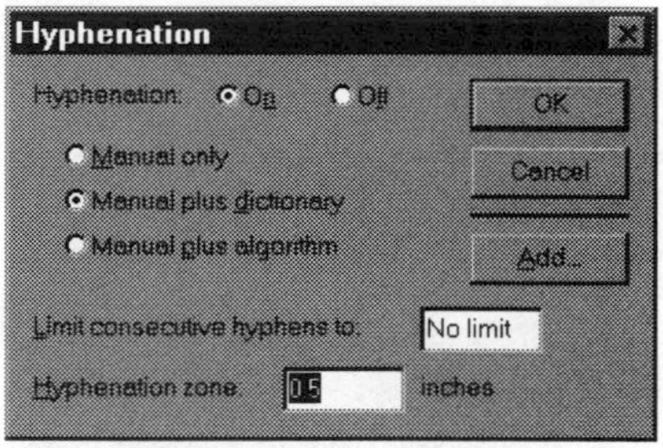

Figure 7 *The Hyphenation dialog box controls hyphenation as a part of the style.*

Adding Hyphenation Characteristics

For each style you create, you can set up different hyphenation specifications. For example, a style used for text in relatively wide text blocks might have a narrower hyphenation zone than the hyphenation settings for another text style.

1 To add hyphenation options to your new style, click the **Hyph** button. PageMaker will display the Hyphenation dialog box **(Figure 7)**.

2 Make whatever changes you want to the dialog box. Remember to click the **On** radio button if you want to turn hyphenation on.

Click OK to return to the Edit Style dialog box.

Defining Styles

Saving the New Style

The last step in creating a new style is to save it before exiting the style dialog boxes. When you are finished with the Edit Style dialog box **(Figure 8)**, choose the OK button to move back to the Define styles dialog box **(Figure 9)**. At this point, if you click the cancel button, none of the new styles, nor any of their characteristics will be saved. To save the information, be sure to click the OK button. PageMaker will return to your document, and your new styles will be displayed in the Styles palette.

Choose OK to save the style you have just configured

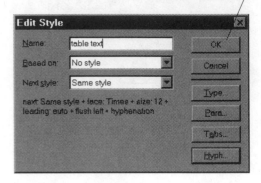

Figure 8 *Click OK to save the work you've just done configuring the new style.*

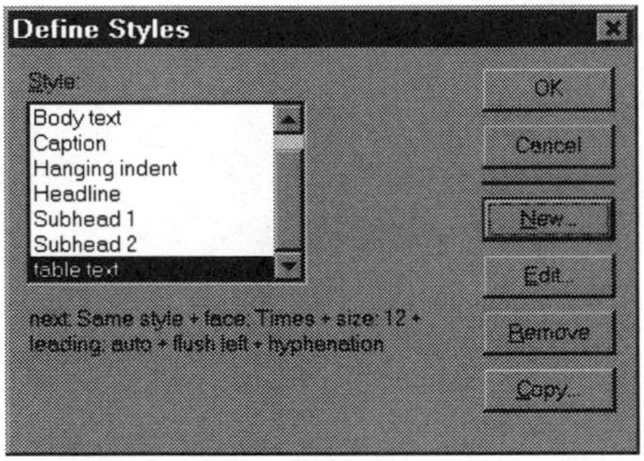

Figure 9 *New style name is added to list of styles in Define Styles dialog box.*

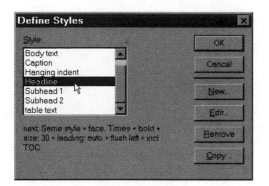

Figure 10 *Choose the style you want to modify and click the Edit button.*

Editing Styles

The procedure to edit an existing style is exactly the same as creating a new style.

1 Open the Type menu and choose the Define Styles command.

2 In the Define Styles dialog box **(Figure 10)**, click the style you want to edit from the list, and choose the **Edit** button.

3 PageMaker will open the same Edit style dialog box we used to define new styles. The different is all the style characteristics have already been defined. Notice the same format description in the dialog box **(Figure 11)**.

4 To modify the style, click the applicable characteristic buttons, and make the needed changes to the style's format.

5 When you are finished modifying the style, choose OK to move back to the Define Styles dialog box, and click OK to save the modifications and return to your document.

Style description shows you the current settings for the style

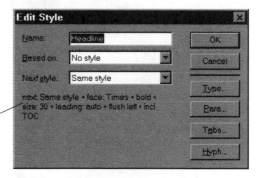

Figure 11 *Use the Edit Style dialog box to make any changes to existing styles.*

Modifying Styles

Copying Styles from Other Documents

PageMaker lets you share styles among documents. The styles you create in one document can be copied to a new document without the drudgery of having to recreate the styles. Here's how:

1 Open the Type menu and choose the Define Styles command.

2 In the Define Styles dialog box **(Figure 12)** click the **Copy** button.

3 PageMaker will open the Copy styles dialog box **(Figure 13)**. Find the folder and PageMaker document whose styles you want to use.

4 Click OK to copy the styles to the document you're currently working in.

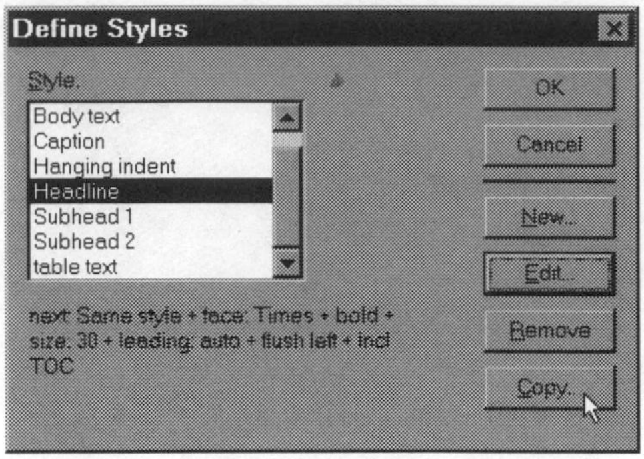

Figure 12 *To copy styles from another document, click the Copy button in the Define Styles dialog box.*

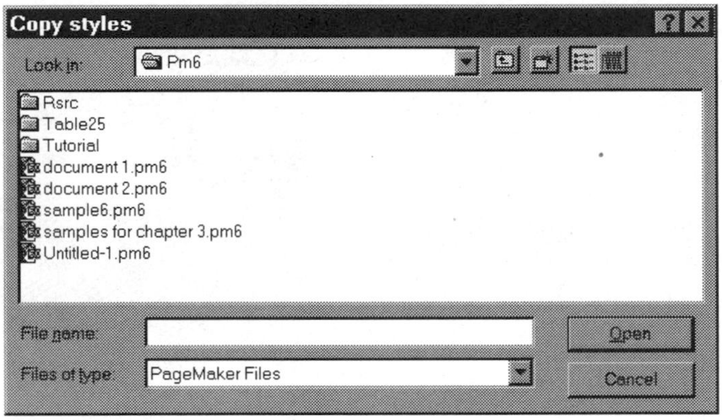

Figure 13 *Find the document whose styles you want to copy in the Copy styles dialog box.*

Copying Styles

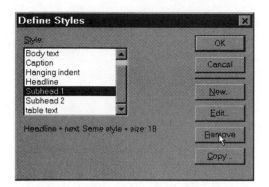

Figure 14 *To delete a style, click the Remove button in the Define Styles dialog box.*

Removing Styles

Removing styles is easy, almost too easy. Be careful because PageMaker fails to ask you if you really want to remove the styles. It just goes ahead and does it—blip and it's gone.

1 Open the Type menu and choose the Define Styles command.

2 In the Define Styles dialog box **(Figure 14)** click the style name you want to delete and click the **Remove** button.

3 PageMaker will delete the style. Text that had been assigned the removed style will be shown in the Styles palette to have No Style.

Deleting Styles

Quick and Easy Work Habits

■ Styles are truly the key to productivity in PageMaker. They are simple to create, easy to modify, quick to copy from other documents. I use style exclusively if I need to design anything more complicated than a business card. As I develop a new design, I always change the style rather than experimenting individually with paragraphs. That way I know I have only the styles to experiment with.

■ A quick shortcut to the Define Styles dialog box is **Ctrl+3**.

■ The best advice I can give about using styles is to really use them. Assign every bit of type in your document to a specific style. Then, if you need to change any specifications, simply change the style and all the text associated with the style will automatically change.

Using Drawing Tools

ONCE YOU HAVE ADDED the necessary text to your document, it's time for some graphic elements to help the text communicate. While PageMaker is certainly no Adobe Illustrator, it does have some simple drawing tools that will create lines, boxes, ellipses, circles, and polygons.

This chapter will explain how to use each of the tools to create lines, boxes, ellipses and polygons on your pages. You will understand how to specify the size of the lines that create the various shapes, and how to fill the inside of closed shapes with color or tints of color. Finally, once you have learned how to create different objects with PageMaker's drawing tools, you will learn how to add and control layers of objects on the page.

Drawing Lines

Use the Line tool to draw straight lines in any orientation you want. If you hold down the Shift key, you can limit the orientation to 45–degree increments (meaning, if you want to be sure you are creating a horizontal line, hold down Shift while you draw it).

1 Click the Line tool in the toolbox **(Figure 1)** and the mouse arrow will change to a cross hair icon **(Figure 2)**.

2 Position the cross hair where you want to begin drawing the line (normally the left starting point for the line).

3 Press the mouse button and drag the cross hair to the right the length of the line and in any up, down or diagonal direction **(Figure 3)**. Release the mouse button when the line is the length you want.

Figure 1 *Line toolbox button.*

Figure 2 *Cross hair indicates a drawing tools is active.*

Figure 3 *Click and drag the cross hair to draw a line with the Line tool.*

Lines

Sizing handles for line

Figure 4 *Clicking the line with the Pointer tool reveals the line's sizing handles.*

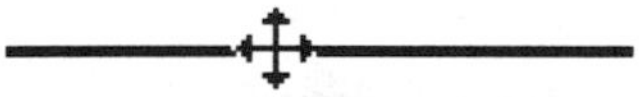

Figure 5 *The four-way arrow drags the line without changing its length.*

Figure 6 *To stretch the line, click a sizing handle and drag.*

Figure 7 *To rotate the line, click either sizing handle and rotate it around the opposite sizing handle.*

Modifying Lines

Once you have drawn a line, or any element with the toolbox tool, it can only be modified with the Pointer tool.

1 Choose the Pointer tool from the toolbox and click the line to reveal its sizing handles **(Figure 4)**.

2 To move the line on the page, click anywhere on the line except on a sizing handle (the pointer will change to a four-way arrow), hold down the mouse button and drag the line to its new position **(Figure 5)**.

3 To stretch either endpoint, click a sizing handle (the pointer will change to a one-sided stretch icon), and drag the handle in or out to resize the line **(Figure 6)**.

4 To change the orientation of the line, click a sizing handle and drag the handle clockwise or counterclockwise to change the amount of rotation **(Figure 7)**.

Lines

Changing Line Specifications

PageMaker's default settings for line specifications may be fine for most of your documents. But it pays to experiment: PageMaker can size line weight from 12 points down to $\frac{1}{4}$ point. To change specifications:

1 Click the line with the Pointer tool to select the line **(Figure 8)**.

2 Click open the Element menu and choose the Line command **(Figure 9)**.

3 Select the size and format you want for your line.

Tips

▪ If you follow these three steps after selecting the Pointer tool, your choices will become the new default setting for lines in your document. To override the default setting, either click the Line tool and change the specifications, or use the Pointer tool to click the individual line you want changed and make the changes.

▪ To change specifications for several lines at once, click the Pointer tool, hold down the Shift key and click the lines. All will be actively selected and the specifications you set will affect all of them.

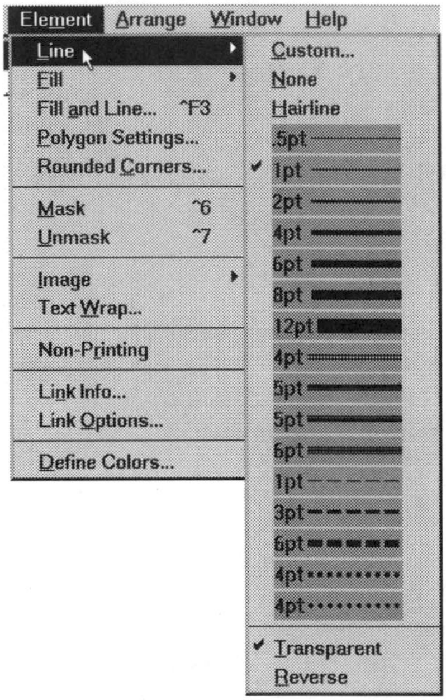

Figure 8 *Sizing handles show that line is selected.*

Element	Arrange	Window	Help
Line ▸		Custom...	
Fill ▸		None	
Fill and Line... ^F3		Hairline	
Polygon Settings...		.5pt	
Rounded Corners...	✓	1pt	
Mask ^6		2pt	
Unmask ^7		4pt	
		6pt	
Image ▸		8pt	
Text Wrap...		12pt	
Non-Printing		4pt	
Link Info...		5pt	
Link Options...		5pt	
Define Colors...		6pt	
		1pt	
		3pt	
		6pt	
		4pt	
		4pt	
	✓	Transparent	
		Reverse	

Figure 9 *Choose the Line command on the Element menu to open the Line submenu.*

Drawing Boxes

While you could build boxes using the Line tool, it's easier and more accurate to use the Rectangle tool. It makes boxes of any size with perfect corners. If you hold down the Shift key while you drag out the box, PageMaker will create a perfect square.

1 Choose the Rectangle tool from the toolbox **(Figure 10)**. The mouse icon will change to a cross hair.

2 Start by positioning the upper left corner of the rectangle. Press the mouse button and drag the cross hair across to create the length, and down to create the width for the box **(Figure 11)**. Release the mouse button when the rectangle is the size you want.

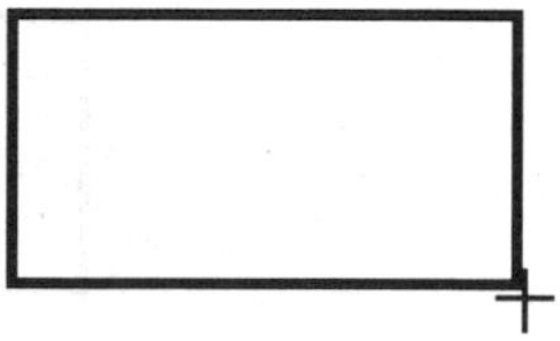

Figure 10 *Rectangle toolbox button.*

Figure 11 *Drag cross hair diagonally to draw a box.*

Boxes

Modifying Boxes

Boxes are changed much the same as lines:

1 Choose the Pointer tool and click the box to select it **(Figure 12)**.

2 To move the box, click on any side, but not on an individual sizing handle. Click and drag the box to a new position **(Figure 13)**.

3 To change a side, click on a side sizing handle and drag **(Figure 14)**.

4 To change two sides at once, click on the corner sizing handle that intersects the two sides you want to change. Click and drag the corner to alter the sides **(Figure 15)**.

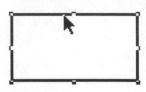

Figure 12 *Clicking anywhere on the box line selects the box.*

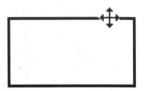

Figure 13 *With box selected, clicking anywhere on the line except a handle moves the box,*

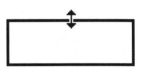

Figure 14 *Clicking a middle sizing handle moves just that side in or out.*

Figure 15 *Clicking a corner handle moves both sides that join the corner.*

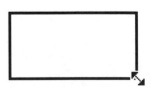

Boxes

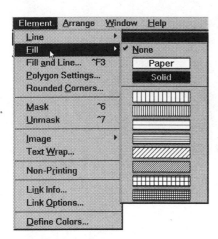

Figure 16 *Choose the Fill command on the Element menu to open the Fill submenu.*

Adding Patterned Fills to Boxes

Just as you can change the weight of lines, you change the weight of the line that creates the rectangle. You can also change the color of the box, called the *fill*. To add a patterned fill to the inside of a box:

1 Choose the Pointer tool and click the box to select it.

2 Open the Element menu and choose the Fill command **(Figure 16)**.

3 In the Fill submenu **(Figure 17)**, choose the pattern you want for the selected box.

4 Choose **Solid** to apply a solid fill color to the box—this is the color ink you are printing your document in, normally black.

5 Choose **Paper** to color the inside of the box the same color as the paper—normally white.

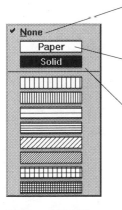

Means box or ellipse is transparent

Means box has same color as paper (white)

Means box has color of ink or printer toner (Black)

Figure 17 *Fill submenu.*

Boxes

Controlling Lines and Fills

Since boxes need the attention of both line and fill specifications, use PageMaker's Fill and Line dialog box to control both at the same time. Let's take a look:

1 Choose the Pointer tool and click the box to select it.

2 Open the Element menu and choose the Fill and Line command to see the Fill and Line dialog box **(Figure 18)**.

3 Now specify the fill and the line—and their color and tint, if any.

▪ **Fill**—The Fill list box shows the same fill pattern as the Fill submenu.

▪ **Line**—The Line list box offers the same line choices as on the Line submenu.

▪ **Color**—Open the color list box and choose one of PageMaker's default colors (you must be able to print using a color printer in order to print these colors).

▪ **Tint**—This list box provides tints, or percentages of solid color. For example, if you select a 10% tint of black, PageMaker will create a 10% screen of black to fill the box with. This will print on your laser printer as a very light gray.

Tip

▪ If you are filling a box with a tint of a color, consider coloring the line the same tint, or remove the line by choosing **None** in the Line list box.

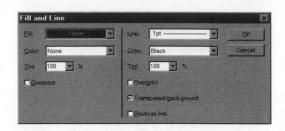

Figure 18 *Fill and Line dialog box lets you specify both the fill and line at the same time.*

Element	Arrange	Win
Line		▶
Fill		▶
Fill and Line...	⌃F3	
Polygon Settings...		
Rounded Corners...		
Mask	⌃6	
Unmask	⌃7	
Image		▶
Text Wrap...		
Non-Printing		
Link Info...		
Link Options...		
Define Colors...		

Figure 19 *Choose the Round Corners command on the Element menu.*

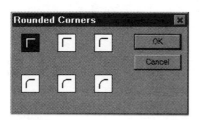

Figure 20 *Specify the radius of corners with the Rounded Corners dialog box.*

Rounding Box Corners

Normal boxes that you draw with the Rectangle tool have sharp, 90-degree corners. For a softer look, consider rounding the corners.

1 Choose the Pointer tool and click the box whose corners you want to round.

2 Click open the Element menu and choose the Rounded Corners command **(Figure 19)**.

3 PageMaker will open the Rounded Corners dialog box **(Figure 20)**. Use this dialog box to define the amount of radius for the corners of the box (i.e., how rounded or sharp the corners will be).

4 Choose OK to return to your document.

Rounding Corners

About Object Layers

PageMaker, as well as most design software, works with layers of objects. One layer might be a color, the second layer over that might be the outline of a box and a third layer might be text inside the box. The ability to layer is one of the important differences between art programs and word processors.

In order to control the stacking order of layers, PageMaker uses several commands found on the Arrange menu **(Figure 21)**.

▪ **Bring to Front**—Moves the selected object to the very front position in the stack (shortcut is **Ctrl+F**).

▪ **Bring Forward**—Moves the selected object forward one layer at a time (shortcut is **Ctrl+8**).

▪ **Send to Back**—Moves the selected object to the bottom or back of the stack (shortcut is **Ctrl+B**).

▪ **Send Backward**—Moves the selected object back one layer at a time (shortcut is **Ctrl+9**).

Tip

▪ When one object is layered in front of another object, hiding the object in back, how do you select the hidden object? Simply choose the Pointer tool, position it outside the boundaries of all objects (including any text block), and click and drag out a selection outline (called a *marquee*) around the objects. When you release the mouse button, all the objects in the layer will be selected, and can be moved together as a group.

Figure 21 *Commands on the arrange menu control object layering.*

Object Layering

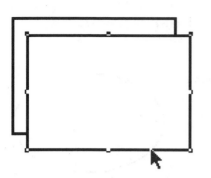

Figure 22 *Copy and paste the box to add the shadow behind it.*

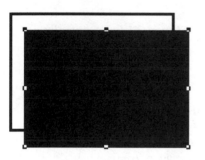

Figure 23 *Moving the "shadow" layer behind the box.*

Creating Drop Shadows

The easiest example of object layering and using the layering commands is to create a simple drop shadow behind a box. The shadow is the layer in back, the box is the layer in the middle and, if you add text in the box, it is the layer in front.

1 Choose the Rectangle tool and draw a rectangle on the page. Now, let's make a copy exactly the same size.

2 Choose the Pointer tool and click the rectangle to select it. Open the Edit menu and choose the Copy command to copy the object. The Choose the Paste command from the same menu to paste the second object over the first.

3 While the second object—the one you just pasted—is still selected, click and drag it a bit to the right and down **(Figure 22)**.

4 Open the Element menu and choose a solid fill for the selected object (it will become the shadow). Then, while it is still selected, press **Ctrl+B** to move it to the back, behind the first box you drew **(Figure 23)**.

5 Notice that you can see the second box—the shadow—through the first box. That's because the first box doesn't yet have a fill—you can see through it. Choose **Paper** from the Fill submenu, add some type in the box, and you have the completed drop shadow box **(Figure 24)**.

Figure 24 *Choose a Paper fill for the top layer to hide all but the shadow of the layer underneath.*

Drop Shadows

Drawing Ellipses and Circles

PageMaker handles ellipses exactly the same as rectangles. To create perfect circles, hold down the Shift key while you drag the cross hair.

1 Choose the Ellipsis tool from the toolbox **(Figure 25)**. The mouse icon will change to a cross hair.

2 Start by positioning the upper left edge of the ellipsis. Press the mouse button and drag the cross hair across and down to create the width and depth for the ellipsis **(Figure 26)**. Release the mouse button when the ellipsis is the size you want.

Creating Polygons

1 Choose the Polygon tool from the toolbox **(Figure 27)**.

2 Start in the upper left area of the polygon, click and drag to the right and down until you get the size you want **(Figure 28)**.

3 PageMaker's default polygon is a pentagon (5 sides). To add more sides, select the polygon, open the Element menu and choose the Polygon Settings command.

4 You will see the Polygon Settings dialog box **(Figure 29)**. Enter the number of sides you want for the selected polygon in the preview area.

5 To add inset midpoints, use the Star inset scroll bar to change the shape as much as you want **(Figure 30)**.

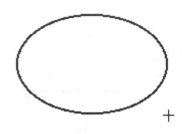

Figure 25 *Ellipse toolbox button.*

Figure 26 *Click and drag the ellipse cross hair diagonally to create the oval.*

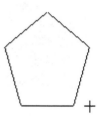

Figure 27 *Polygon toolbox button.*

Figure 28 *Click and drag the Polygon cross hair diagonally to create the polygon.*

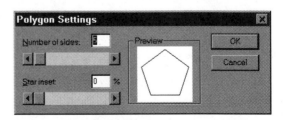

Figure 29 *Polygon Settings dialog box.*

Figure 30 *Star inset feature breaks the five sides into multiple points.*

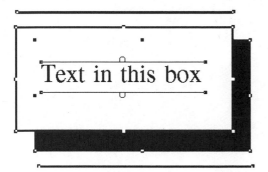

Figure 31 *Each object's sizing handles are selected by shift-clicking the objects.*

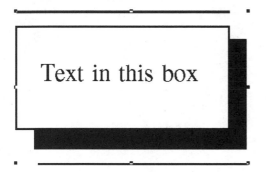

Figure 32 *Note sizing handles around the grouped objects.*

Grouping and Ungrouping Objects

Once you have created a layered object, you must select all layers in order to move the design as a group. Rather than take the trouble to always remember to drag out a marquee around the objects you want moved as a group, just group them together.

1 Choose the Pointer tool from the toolbox.

2 Hold down the Shift key and click each object you want to include in the group.

3 When all the items are selected **(Figure 31)**, open the Arrange menu and choose the Group command (or use the shortcut **Ctrl+G**).

4 PageMaker will lock each selected item together as a single item, with one set of sizing handles around the periphery of the group **(Figure 32)**.

5 Size the group as you would a single object. Text in text blocks that are a part of the group can still be modified with the Type Specifications dialog box, as if there was an independent block of text. Simply highlight with the Text tool and make whatever modifications you want.

6 To ungroup the objects, select the group with the Pointer tool and choose the Ungroup command on the Arrange menu (or use the shortcut **Ctrl+U**).

Grouping Objects

Quick and Easy Work Habits

▪ Get comfortable using the layering shortcuts **Ctrl+B** for move behind, and **Ctrl+F** for move up front. They are invaluable when working quickly with PageMaker.

▪ Likewise, remember to note what the default line and fill settings are prior to creating lines, boxes, ellipses, and polygons. Make the line and fill selection first with the pointer tool and you won't have to worry about changing each shape you create.

▪ The Group and Ungroup commands on the Arrange menu are a big improvement. If you have worked with version 5.0 and fallen prey to the additions PS Group It and PS Ungroup It, you have learned that those additions were your worst nightmare. The two additions still exist in the form of Plug-ins. Stay clear of them and use the commands on the Arrange menu instead.

Quick Work Tips

Adding Graphic Images

THE MOST SATISFYING OF PageMaker's features is its ability to import color photographs onto the pages of your document. Not only can PageMaker display those photos, but it can generate the color separations for color photos that your commercial printer can print. PageMaker's graphic abilities mean that you are no longer required to run to a custom color separator to produce part of your color jobs. Separating color graphics is described in Chapter 12.

Based on the graphic import filters you installed when you installed PageMaker, there are a variety of different formats that PageMaker supports, including TIFF (tagged-image file format), EPS (encapsulated PostScript files), Kodak Photo CD files, MacPaint, PICT, Scitex CT files, AutoCAD DXF, CompuServe GIF, PC PaintBrush, and Windows Metafiles.

Importing Graphics

To import a graphic file, you place the image exactly the way you learned to place text in Chapter 3.

1 Move to the page you want to add a graphic to.

2 Click open the File menu and choose the Place command **(Figure 1)**.

3 PageMaker will open the Place document dialog box **(Figure 2)**.

4 Now, find the graphic file you want to import. Use the navigation buttons to move to the folder holding the graphic. Remember, PageMaker will recognize only those types of graphics you have installed import filters for.

5 Click OK to import the graphic and place it on the page.

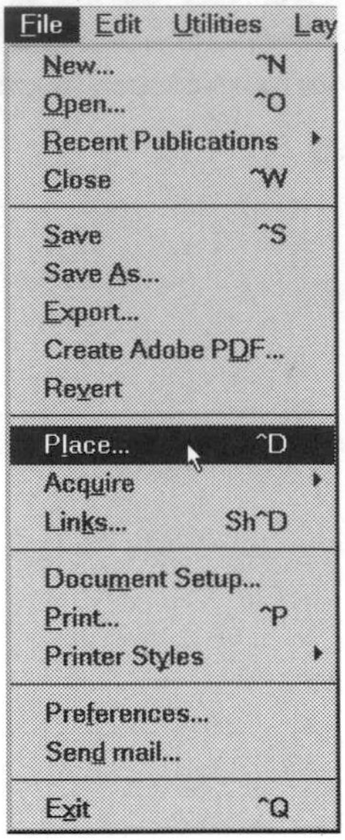

Tips

■ To make a graphic part of the text block (called an *inline* graphic), choose the Text tool and click in the text block where you want to add the graphic. Then open the Place document dialog box. Be sure to click the **As inline graphic** radio button.

■ A quick shortcut to the Place document dialog box is **Ctrl+D**.

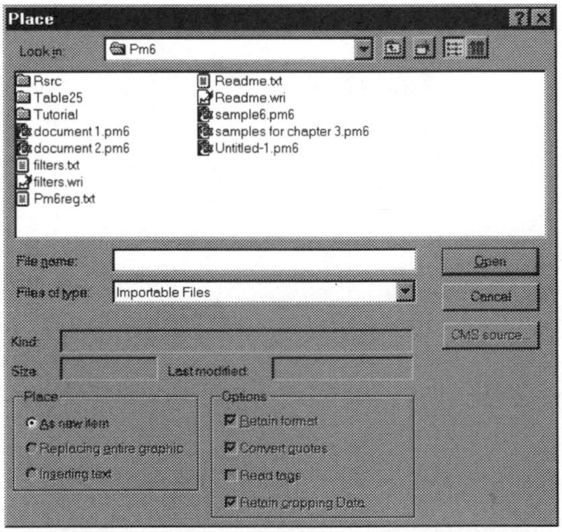

Figure 1 *Choose the Place command on the File menu.*

Figure 2 *Use the Place document dialog box to import graphic files.*

Figure 3 *Click the graphic to display its sizing handles.*

Figure 4 *Click the graphic other than on a sizing handle and drag to position.*

Positioning Graphics on the Page

Using the Place document dialog box simply gets the graphic onto the page. Now, it's up to you to position it where you want it.

1 Choose the Pointer tool from the toolbox.

2 Click the graphic to select it—the sizing handles will appear **(Figure 3)**.

3 Click the mouse arrow anywhere on the graphic except on a sizing handle and drag the graphic to position it where you want **(Figure 4)**.

Tip

■ You may want to add some guides to help align the graphic; then drag the graphic and let it snap to the guides.

Sizing Graphics

1 Choose the Pointer tool from the tool-box.

2 Click the graphic to select it—the sizing handles will appear **(Figure 5)**.

3 Drag either side handle to shrink or stretch that side **(Figure 6)**. Drag a top or bottom handle to shrink or stretch the top or bottom.

4 Click a corner handle to change the dimensions of the two sides forming the corner.

5 To size the graphic proportionally, Shift-click a corner handle and shrink or stretch the graphic proportionally **(Figure 7)**.

Figure 5 *Click the graphic to display its sizing handles.*

Figure 6 *Dragging any side handle stretches or shrinks that side.*

Figure 7 *Drag a corner handle while holding down the Shift key to size graphic proportionally.*

Cropping Graphics

Instead of shrinking or stretching the graphic, you might want to just trim some of it away. Use the Cropping tool in the toolbox.

Figure 8 *Cropping toolbox button.*

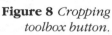

1 Choose the Cropping tool in the toolbox **(Figure 8)**.

2 Click the graphic with the Cropping tool to display the sizing handles **(Figure 9)**.

3 Click any sizing handle and drag the handle inward to crop away the unwanted area of the graphic **(Figure 10)**. You can use the Cropping tool at any time to drag the side that was cropped away back to its original size.

Figure 9 *Click the graphic to reveal its sizing handles.*

Figure 10 *Click a sizing handle with the cropping tool and drag it to crop portions of the graphic.*

Cropping Graphics

Placing Inline Graphics

Inline graphics become part of the text block. They are locked in relative position to the surrounding text and move with the text. Inline graphics are placed identically to independent graphics. The difference is that you must first choose the Text tool and click the text insertion point in a text box at the position you want the graphic.

1 Move to the page you want to add a graphic to.

2 Choose the Text tool from the toolbox and click the text insertion point in a text box where you want to position the inline graphic.

3 Click open the File menu and choose the Place command.

4 PageMaker will open the Place document dialog box **(Figure 11)**.

5 Find the graphic file you want to import. Use the navigation buttons to move to the folder holding the graphic.

6 Be sure that the **As inline graphic** radio button is clicked **(Figure 12)**.

7 Click OK to import the graphic and place it in the text box **(Figure 13)**.

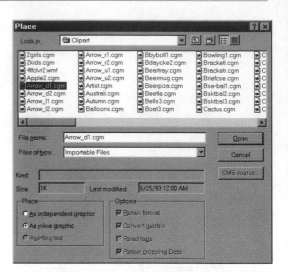

Figure 11 *Use the Place document dialog box to import inline graphics.*

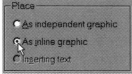

Figure 12 *Confirm that you are importing a graphic inline by clicking the As inline graphic button.*

Driving in snow can be a harrowing experience if you've never done it before. It takes skill, a knowledge of physics and nerves of steel to learn the proper technique.

Figure 13 *Graphic is placed as a part of the text block (inline) as opposed to an independent object on the page.*

Inline Graphics

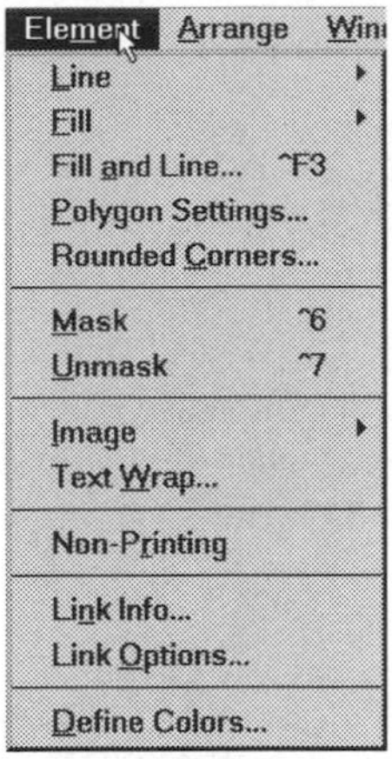

Adjusting Image Quality

PageMaker allows limited enhancements to grayscale TIFF graphic images. You can make very basic changes to contrast and brightness, and change the dot shape for screened images.

To adjust an image:

1 Choose the Pointer tool and click the graphic you want to modify.

2 Open the Element menu and choose the Image command **(Figure 14)**, to open the Image submenu **(Figure 15)**.

3 Choose Image Control to open the Image control dialog box **(Figure 16)**.

4 Use the tools in the dialog box to make changes to the image quality.

5 Click **Apply** to preview the changes to the graphic (you might have to drag the dialog box over to see the graphic underneath).

6 To go back to the original image settings, click **Reset**.

Figure 14 *Choose the Image command on the Element menu.*

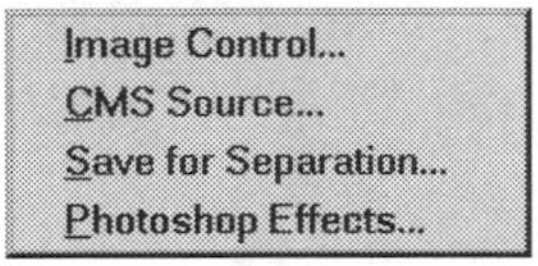

Figure 15 *Image submenu.*

Image Quality

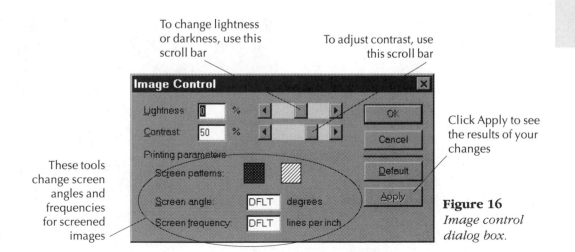

To change lightness or darkness, use this scroll bar

To adjust contrast, use this scroll bar

Click Apply to see the results of your changes

These tools change screen angles and frequencies for screened images

Figure 16 *Image control dialog box.*

Controlling the Display of Graphics

Some graphic files, such as color TIFF files, are extremely large, and may significantly slow down your computer's ability to scroll across the page. You can reduce the resolution at which graphics are displayed. Here's how:

1 Click open the File menu and choose the Preferences command **(Figure 17)**.

2 PageMaker will open the Preferences dialog box **(Figure 18)**.

3 Look in the Graphics display area to see which display resolution is set. If high resolution is set, you can click Standard to reduce the resolution and still see the display of the page. Standard resolution is good enough to see a rendering of the graphic. If Standard resolution is set, you can further reduce the display resolution by choosing Gray out, which will display graphics as gray colored boxes.

Tip

▪ Regardless of the display resolution set, the resolution that PageMaker will use to print the page is not reduced by the preference setting.

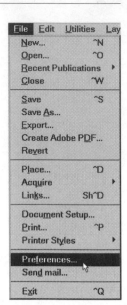

Figure 17 *Choose the Preferences command on the File menu.*

Click to adjust the resolution of displayed graphics ———

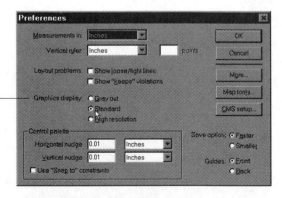

Figure 18 *Speed up the display of graphics by choosing a lower resolution option in the Preferences dialog box.*

Display Resolution

Driving in snow harrowing experience if you done it before. It takes skill

Figure 19 *Select the object you want to make "non-printing."*

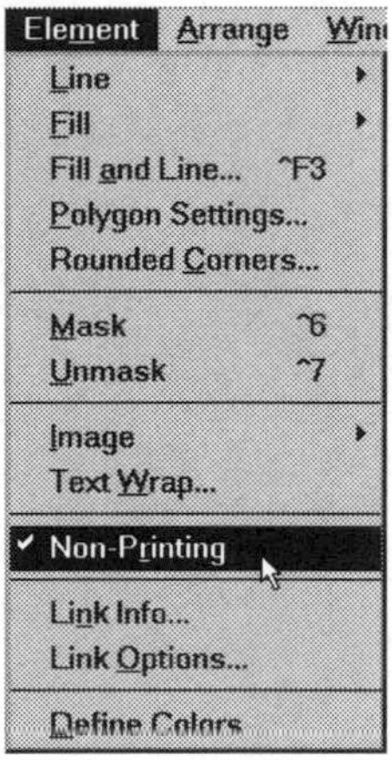

Element Arrange Win
Line
Fill
Fill and Line... ^F3
Polygon Settings...
Rounded Corners...
Mask ^6
Unmask ^7
Image
Text Wrap...
✓ Non-Printing
Link Info...
Link Options...
Define Colors

Figure 20 *Choose the Non-Printing command on the Element menu.*

Making Items Non-Printing

To mark any object on the page as a non-printing object:

1 Click the object with the Pointer tool **(Figure 19)**.

2 Click open the Element menu and choose the Non-Printing command **(Figure 20)**.

3 The sizing handles on the selected item will change from black to the same non-repro blue as the guides.

4 To return the non-printing object to its normal, printable status, select the item with the Pointer tool and choose the command a second time to remove the check mark.

Tips

▪ Marking graphics as non-printing objects is handy when you want a quick print of the document pages and don't want to wait for the graphics to print. Just remember to make the object printable again when you are ready for your final print run.

▪ If you need a quick print of everything on your pages, including those items you made non-printing, choose the **Ignore non-printing settings** check box in the Print Document dialog box.

Non-Printing Graphics

Saving Graphics in Libraries

Libraries are permanent storage areas for anything you need and use in PageMaker. You might use one library to store scanned client logos, another library might hold boilerplate text, and a third could hold product codes, or catalog descriptions. While libraries act a lot like basic folders, it's much easier to add library contents to your pages. Let's take a look:

1 Click open the Window menu and choose the Library command. PageMaker will display the Open library dialog box **(Figure 21)**.

2 Enter a name for the library you want. If you are creating a new library, enter the name you want for the library and click the **Open** button. PageMaker will display a warning that you are about to create a new library **(Figure 22)**. Click **Yes**.

3 PageMaker will open the new library **(Figure 23)**.

4 To add any item to a library, simply click the item with the Pointer tool to select it and click the add (plus) button in the library dialog box.

5 To move an item stored in the library onto the page, simply click the item and drag it to the position you want.

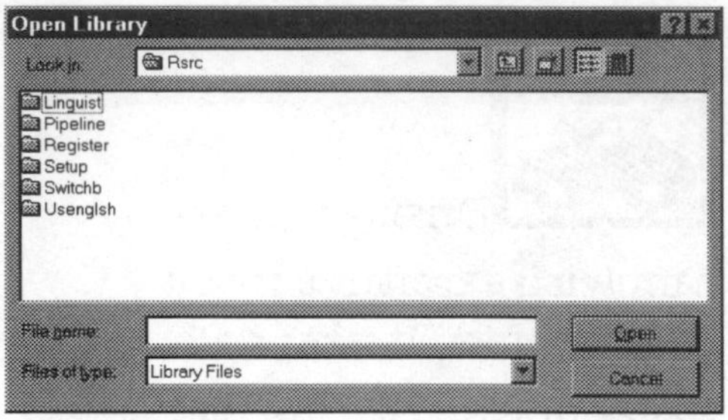

Figure 21 *Open library dialog box show available libraries and lets you create new libraries.*

Figure 22 *PageMaker warns you that you about to create a new library.*

Figure 23 *Newly created library.*

Figure 24 *Click graphic with Rotation tool to select it.*

Figure 25 *Drag a rotation arm out from the center of the graphic.*

Figure 26 *Use the rotation arm as a lever to rotate the graphic in either direction.*

Rotating Graphics

1 Choose the Rotation tool from the toolbox and click the graphic to highlight it **(Figure 24)**.

2 Position the rotation icon in the center of the graphic, click and drag a rotation arm to the right **(Figure 25)**.

3 Now, while still holding down the mouse button, rotate the arm up or down to turn the graphic on the center point counterclockwise or clockwise **(Figure 26)**.

4 To rotate a graphic using the Control palette, click the graphic with the Pointer tool and enter the degrees of rotation in the rotation text box **(Figure 27)**.

Tip

■ Rotate the graphic with the Control palette counterclockwise by entering a positive number, or clockwise with a negative number.

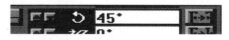

Figure 27 *Using the Control palette, enter the number of degrees of rotation in the rotation text box.*

Rotating Graphics

Skewing Graphics

1 Click the graphic with the Pointer tool to select it **(Figure 28)**.

2 Enter the degrees of skew in the skew text box of the Control palette **(Figure 29)**. Positive numbers skew the graphic to the right, while negative numbers force the graphic to lean to the left **(Figure 30)**.

Figure 28 *Select the graphic with the Pointer tool.*

Figure 29 *Enter the number of degrees of skew in the skew text box.*

Figure 30 *The skewed graphic with 25 degrees of positive skew.*

Adding Color

PAGEMAKER CAN HANDLE ALL your color needs with aplomb. It is capable of applying color to any object, be it text or graphic. It can handle color photos that have been enhanced with a program like Adobe Photoshop and placed in PageMaker. Furthermore it can separate those photos into individual cyan, magenta, yellow, and black process plates for color process printing (see Chapter 12 for more information about color separations). PageMaker can just as easily work with spot color, and contains a number of color models, chief among them Pantone's color matching system, that you can use to specify an exact match of spot ink. Finally, PageMaker's Color Matching System can standardize the *transmitted* color you see on your monitor, with the *reflected* color you see on your printed pages, so that you can have a fairly accurate idea of what your printed results will look like. PageMaker's color capabilities are straightforward, accurate, and easy to learn and use.

Introduction

Opening the Colors palette

1 Click open the Window menu and choose the Colors command (**Figure 1**).

2 PageMaker will display the Colors palette (**Figure 2**). Note the default colors that PageMaker provides.

3 To color objects other than text, click the line, fill or both buttons and choose the color or tint that you want.

4 To color text, choose the color and select a tint (100% is the solid color).

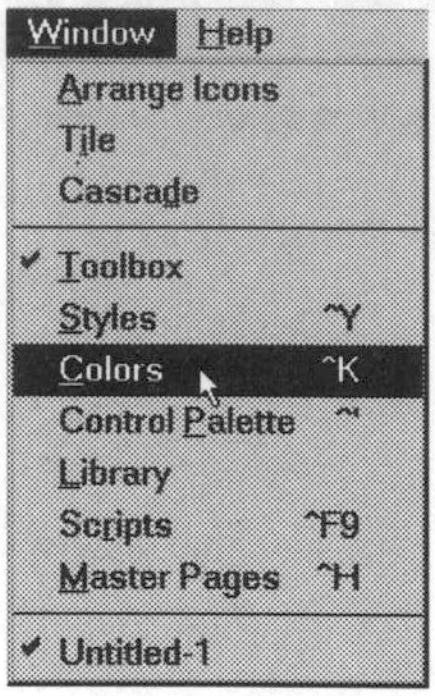

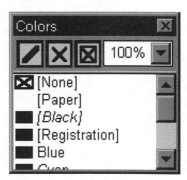

Figure 1 *Choose the Colors command on the Window menu.*

Figure 2 *Apply colors to objects with the Colors palette.*

Color Palette

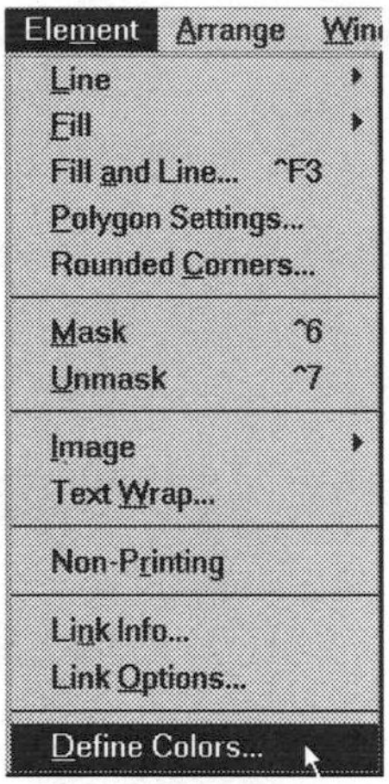

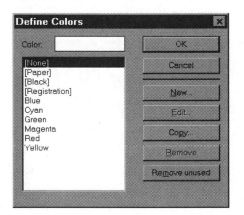

Figure 3 *Choose the Define Colors command on the Element menu.*

Figure 4 *Define Colors dialog box shows existing defined colors and lets you create new colors.*

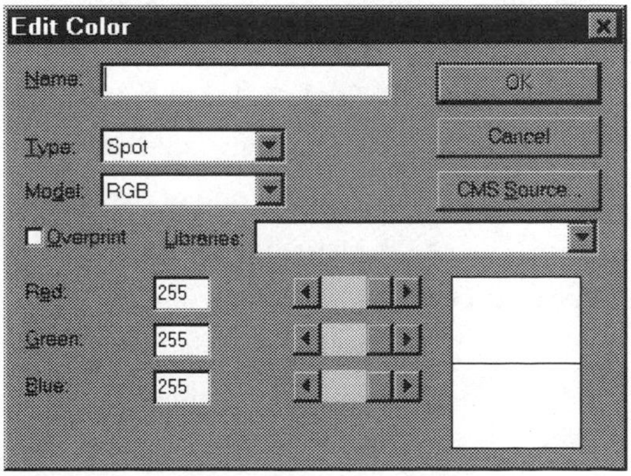

Figure 5 *Create new colors and modify existing colors with the Edit Color dialog box.*

Defining Color

If PageMaker's default colors are not sufficient, you must define the exact colors that you want prior to applying them.

1 Click open the Element menu and choose the Define Colors command **(Figure 3)**.

2 PageMaker will open the Define Colors dialog box **(Figure 4)**.

3 Choose the **New** command to open the Edit Color dialog box **(Figure 5)**.

4 Type a name for the color in the Name text box (if you are selecting a spot color from one of PageMaker's many color libraries, such as the Pantone library, the color number will automatically be added in the Name field).

5 Enter the type of color: **Spot** or **Process**. Spot color is usually a separate color ink mixed to the exact shade that you need. Spot colors are more exactly matched, but costlier to print. Process color is composed of some percentage of the four process colors cyan, magenta, yellow and black. Process colors is the method for printing color photos, and any additional colors defined as process are essentially printed for free. Choose **Tint** if you want to define a percentage tint of a spot or process color.

Defining Color

Choosing a Color Model

1 Click open the Model list box in the Edit Color dialog box **(Figure 6)**. You can choose among RGB, HLS or CMYK.

2 If you want a commercial printer to reproduce your color document, you must select the **CMYK** color model. CMYK stands for the four process colors—cyan, magenta, yellow and black—noted on the previous page. Commercial printers understand and work with process color daily. Use the color slide bars, or enter the exact proportions for each primary color. The preview box shows the developing color interactively.

3 Choose **RGB (Figure 7)** if you will be printing your document on a color printer, such as a color ink jet, dye sublimation, or color laser printer. RGB stands for red, green, blue—colors used by your computer monitor to reproduce color. Your commercial printer cannot print color based on an RGB model.

4 Choose **HLS (Figure 8)** if you are basing color definition on a color wheel model that uses lightness (or brightness) as a defining element of color. HLS stands for hue, lightness and saturation.

Spot Versus Process Color

What are the sorts of jobs you would print with either spot color or process color?

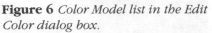

Figure 6 *Color Model list in the Edit Color dialog box.*

Figure 7 *RGB color model.*

Figure 8 *HLS color model.*

Spot color	Printing a simple color (like adding a color rule to a business card)
	Printing metallic colors (gold, silver, bronze or copper)
	Printing one or two colors on a brochure or marketing flyer
	Matching a very specific color
Process color	Printing documents with color photos
	Printing flesh tones
	Printing a number of different colors
	Printing individual colors cyan, magenta, yellow; or tints of those colors

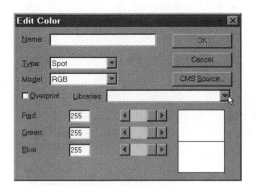

Figure 9 *Click the Libraries menu to see the available color libraries.*

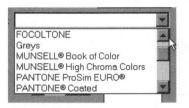

Figure 10 *Scroll down the menu to find the library you want to use.*

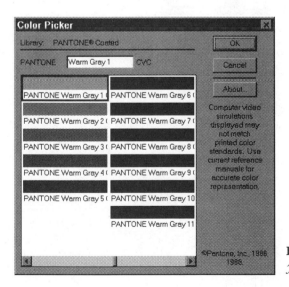

Figure 11 *Color Picker dialog box lets you choose a Pantone color.*

Choosing Pantone Colors

If you want to add one or more spot colors to your document, you will almost certainly choose one of the Pantone libraries. Pantone is a leading manufacturer of ink, and its Pantone Matching System is used extensively by small and large commercial printers.

1 In the Edit Color dialog box **(Figure 9)**, click the libraries arrow to open the Libraries list box **(Figure 10)**.

2 Scroll down the list to see Pantone Coated and Pantone Uncoated. (The coated and uncoated refers to whether your document will be printed on coated or uncoated paper.)

3 Scroll through the color list **(Figure 11)** to find the color you want.

Tip

■ Don't be too trusting of the colors in the Pantone list, or any of the other color models. The actual colors shown are dependent on the color capabilities of your computer, its video graphics adapter and your color monitor. While PageMaker has made great strides in standardizing colors between the monitor and the printed page (PageMaker's Color Matching System is explained later in this chapter), there will still be subtle differences. To ensure you have the right color, double check using the *Pantone Matching System Color Formula Guide*, a printed equivalent of PageMaker's Pantone library.

Pantone Colors

Choosing Process Colors

1   Open the Edit Color dialog box **(Figure 12)**.

2   Choose the CMYK model in the Model list box.

3   Use the slide bars to set percentages of cyan, magenta, yellow and black to create the color you want. The color is previewed in the preview window.

4   Take care that the total percentage of color does not exceed 240%, or the color will become too dark and muddy to print clearly.

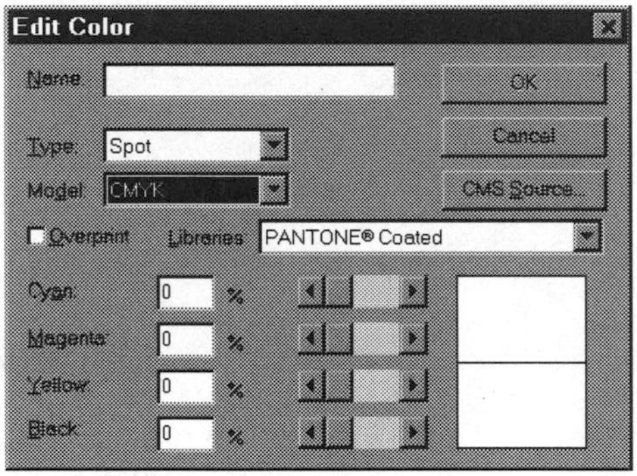

Figure 12 *Choose process colors using the Edit Color dialog box.*

About PageMaker's Color Management System

The Color Management System is an effort by Adobe to standardize color on the monitor with printed color—two totally different kinds of color that actually have no similarities. The color shown on your computer's monitor is transmitted color, based on an *additive* color model—starting with white, the primary colors red, green and blue (RGB) are added in different intensities to create the colors displayed on your monitor. While RGB are the primary mixing colors for transmitted color, printed color is reflected off the page. It is based on an opposite *subtractive* color system, with entirely different primary colors—cyan, magenta, yellow and black (CMYK), called *process* colors. If you plan to have a commercial printer print your document, color must be defined in a subtractive system either as spot color or process color.

Because transmitted and reflected colors are based on entirely different primary colors, you normally cannot duplicate a printed color on a computer's color monitor. PageMaker's Color Management System standardizes the two colors so you can more accurately proof your work. Choose the source for the color you wish to standardize using the Color Management System Source Profile dialog box **(Figure 13)**.

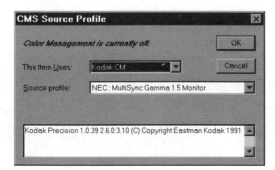

Figure 13 *Color Management System Source Profile dialog box.*

Color Management System

Using the Colors Palette

Once you have defined the colors for your document, it's a simple matter to apply them to text and graphics on the page.

1 Open the Colors palette by clicking the Window command and choosing the Colors command. PageMaker will display the palette **(Figure 14)**. Notice that the palette contains all the colors you have defined for your document.

2 Now, click the object you want to assign a color from the palette. To color text, you must first highlight the text with the text tool.

3 To color the fill of a box or ellipse, first click the fill button, then choose the color and percentage of tint.

4 To color a line, first click the line button, then choose the color.

5 To apply the same color to a lined box or ellipse and its fill, choose the **Both** button and pick the color.

Figure 14 *Colors palette.*

Using the Color Palette

About Trapping

Trapping is probably the least understood aspect of color printing. It is a very detailed process to prevent the accidental misalignment of one color printing on top of a different color. Previous versions of PageMaker lacked a straightforward means to control trapping and was justifiably criticized for it. While Version 6.0 offers a trapping dialog box **(Figure 15)**, I strongly suggest caution to beginning desktop publishers: trapping, or lack of correct trapping, is a printing problem, not a design problem, and is only required to compensate for a potential lack of accuracy in commercial printing presses. If you plan to have a commercial printer duplicate your color document, discuss trapping with your printer before trapping the colors yourself. If you forge ahead and blindly trap colors without consulting your printer, you will likely set trapping values that are not only useless but may require rework by your printer and cost you more to produce the job.

Click here to activate trapping

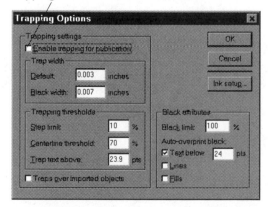

Figure 15 *Trapping Options dialog box handles custom traps.*

Quick and Easy Work Habits

▪ Where possible, specify process colors instead of spot colors. Each time you add a spot color, it requires another run through the printing press. If you have a process color job (four process colors) plus two spot colors, printed on a 2-color press, that's three passes through the press. If you add an additional spot color, that's a fourth time through the press. You can see that spot colors can drastically increase the cost of your job.

▪ Some colors simply look better as spot colors rather than part of the process colors. Metallic colors—gold, silver, bronze and so forth—don't look very authentic when printed as a part of the process plates. You really need to mix metallic-colored ink as additional spot colors to print metallic colors properly.

▪ While it is theoretically possible to get the same exact color whether it is printed as a part of the process colors or as a specially mixed spot color, in practice the colors never look the same. So if you have specified a spot color in your document use it consistently as a spot color; don't try to mix and match process and spot colors on the same page.

Printing

11

IT ISN'T UNTIL DOCUMENTS are printed that you can see the real genius of your designs. The monitor gives you only a rough guess at what the pages look like, displaying graphics and screened tints at less than 100 dots per inch. Yet, even a measly 300 dpi printer can give you a realistic view of your work, and a 600 or 1200 dpi laser printer can make your efforts downright beautiful.

PageMaker's Print Document dialog box is your print control center. The dialog box consists of four or five dialog boxes, each designed to oversee specific details of printing your work. Here you can specify the number of copies and the exact pages you want printed, choose the right paper size pulled from the right paper tray, even create PostScript files that can be sent to prepress service bureaus.

PageMaker and your PC manage the chores of printing without fuss or bother. Click the Print button and PageMaker will download your document to your printer, and immediately let you get back to work. Meanwhile, your computer will feed data to the printer, and your printer will churn out pages as quickly as its memory and processor allow.

Introduction

Getting Ready to Print

There are several chores to do prior to printing your document.

1 To control the starting number of page numbers, open the Document Setup dialog box on the File menu **(Figure 1)**.

2 In the page numbering area, enter the starting page number of the first page of your document in the **Start page #** text box. Normally, this is set to 1, but if you have developed individual chapters for a book, or articles for a magazine, then the starting page number would be different for each chapter or article.

To restart the page numbering, so that page number is not consecutive, click the **Restart page numbering** check box and enter the number you want to restart with in the **Start page #** text box.

3 To change the numbering style for page numbers, click the **Numbers** button to open the Page Numbering dialog box **(Figure 2)**. Choose the style you want from the list of options.

4 To check the status of links to text and graphic files, choose the Links command on the File menu to open the Links dialog box **(Figure 3)**.

5 The status of each link is reported in the Status area. Click **Update** to update links whose status indicates needing updating.

Tip

▪ If you have forgotten to set the resolution for your document, do so now. Open the Document Setup dialog box and choose the resolution you want from the Target printer resolution menu **(Figure 4)**.

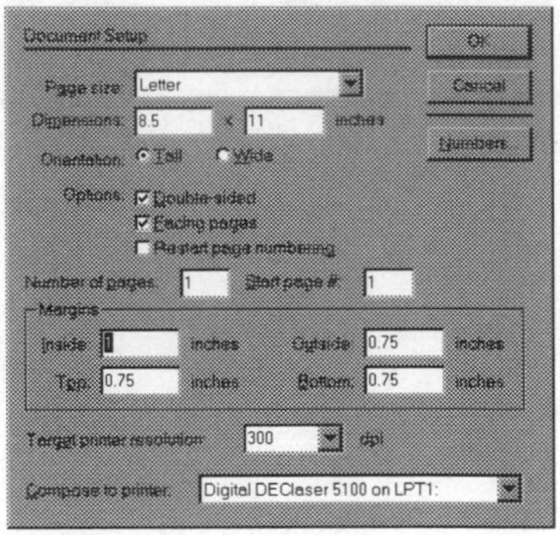

Figure 1 *Document Setup dialog box controls page numbering.*

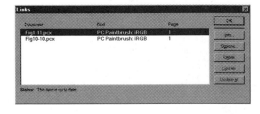

Figure 2 *Choose a numbering style with the Page Numbering dialog box.*

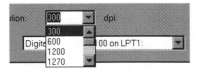

Figure 3 *Check the status of any linked files with the Links dialog box.*

Figure 4 *Set the printer resolution in the Document Setup dialog box.*

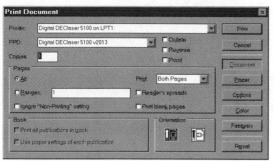

Figure 5 *Choose the printer you want to use in the Print Document dialog box.*

Choosing the Printer

1 Choose the Print command on the File menu to open the Print Document dialog box **(Figure 5)**.

2 Click open the Printer list box and choose the printer you want for this print job **(Figure 6)**.

3 Then, select the PostScript Printer Description (PPD) you want for the printer **(Figure 7)**.

4 Finally, click the **Features** button and select the printing features you want to use for the print job **(Figure 8)**.

Printer:	KODAK ColorEase PS Printer on LPT1:
	HP LaserJet 4 on LPT1:
PPD:	KODAK ColorEase PS Printer on LPT1:
	FX-WORKS on COM2:
Copies:	Digital DEClaser 5100 on LPT1:

Figure 6 *Pick the printer you want from the Printer list box (all installed printers will be shown in the list).*

PPD:	Linotronic 630_630P v52.3
	Linotronic 300 v52.3
Copies:	Linotronic 330 v52.3
	Linotronic 530 v52.3
Pages	Linotronic 630_630P v52.3
All	Linotronic 830 v52.3

Figure 7 *Then, select the PPD you want to use for the printer (each PostScript printer will have a corresponding PPD).*

DECimage Plus Sharpness:

Printer's default
Printer's default
DECSharp
Off
Very Sharp
Extra Sharp

DECimage Plus Punch:

Figure 8 *Finally, choose any special printer settings by clicking the features button and selecting the feature (DEC sharpness enhancement options shown).*

Printing Your Document

1 Choose the Print command on the File menu to open the Print Document dialog box **(Figure 9)**.

2 Choose the PostScript Printer Description for the printer you want to print to, if different than the default PPD shown in the dialog box.

3 Choose the number of copies you want to make of your document. Enter the number in the **Copies** text box.

4 Choose the range of pages you want to print. For example, to print pages 2,3,4,5,8,11,14,15,16,17, and 18, enter the range 2-5, the individual pages 8,11 and the range 14-18 in the text box **(Figure 10)**. To print all the pages in your document, click **All**.

5 Click the **Print** command button to begin printing.

Choose the PPD you want to use for printing —

Then, enter the number of copies you want of each page

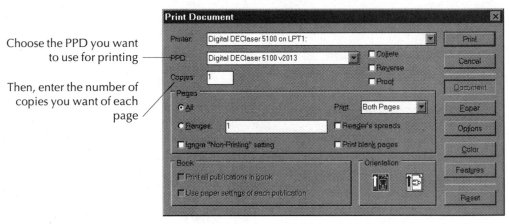

Figure 9 *Print Document dialog box.*

Figure 10 *How to print ranges of pages within a document.*

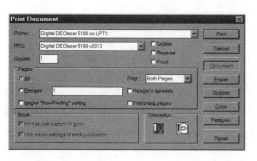

Figure 11 *Print Document dialog box.*

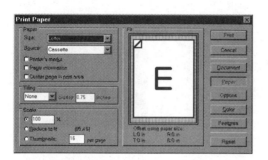

Figure 12 *Set the size of paper with the Print Paper dialog box .*

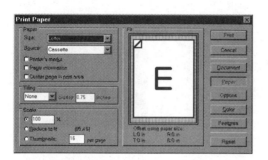

Figure 13 *Select the paper size from the paper menu.*

Setting the Paper Size

Remember back in Chapter 2 when we talked about the difference between the designed page size and the printed page size? Well, now is the time to tell PageMaker what size paper is physically running through your printer—which again, may be a different dimension than the page size you have designed.

1 Choose the Print command on the File menu to open the Print Document dialog box **(Figure 11)**.

2 Click **Paper** to open the Print Paper dialog box **(Figure 12)**.

3 Look in the Paper area of the dialog box and choose a page size from the **Size** menu **(Figure 13)**. Source refers to where the paper is stored in your printer. Open the menu and choose the source for the page size you selected.

4 If you want to see crop marks and registration bullets, click the **Printer's marks** check box. To have the file name, date and time of printing, and separation color names printed at the bottom of your pages, click the **Page information** check box.

Tip

■ If you try to print crop marks and registration bullets only to have PageMaker warn you that they will not fit on the selected paper size, try reducing the size of the printed page. This occurs when the designed page size is the same as the printed page size—there's no room left to add crop marks outside the trim area of the page. So click the **Reduce to fit** button and PageMaker will shrink the page enough to fit the marks on the paper.

Paper Size

Choosing the Printed Page Orientation

Orientation means the manner in which the image is printed on the page, either aligned with the long side (called *portrait*) or with a short side (called *landscape*).

1 Choose the Print command on the File menu to open the Print Document dialog **(Figure 14)**.

2 In the Orientation area **(Figure 15)**, click the orientation you want for this document.

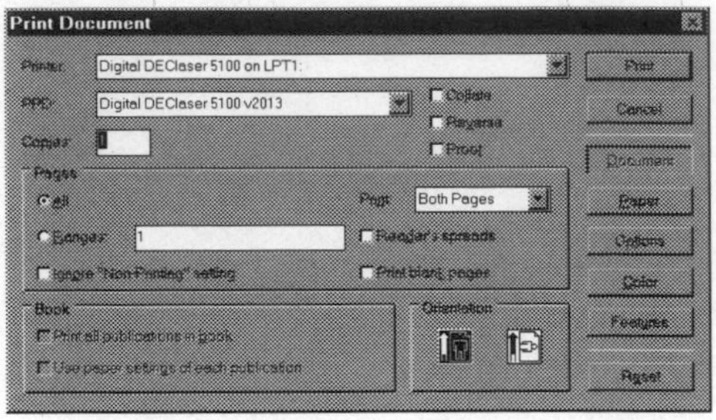

Tip

■ The orientation you choose in the Print Document dialog box should generally match the orientation you set up in the Document Setup dialog box **(Figure 16)**.

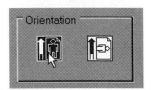

Figure 14 *Print Document dialog box.*

Figure 15 *Select either portrait or landscape orientation. Here portrait is selected.*

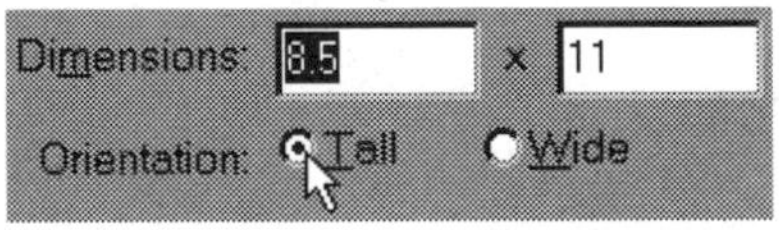

Figure 16 *Orientation in the Print Document dialog box should be the same as in the Document Setup dialog box. Here Tall (portrait) is selected.*

Page Orientation

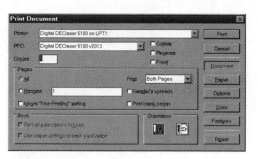

Figure 17 *Print Document dialog box.*

Print: Even Pages

☐ Read Both Pages
Even Pages
Odd Pages

☐ Print blank pages

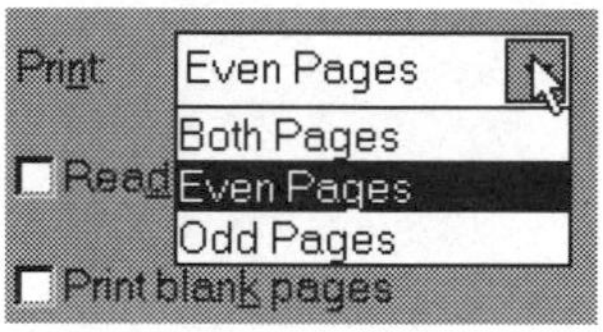

Figure 18 *Use the options on the Print menu to print on both sides of the paper.*

Printing on Both Sides of the Page

Many of today's laser printers are capable of duplex printing—printing on both sides of the paper. If your printer lacks duplex capability, you can still print on both sides, it just takes a moment longer.

1 Choose the Print command on the File menu to open the Print Document dialog box **(Figure 17)**.

2 Open the Print menu **(Figure 18)** and choose **Odd pages**.

3 Click the **Reverse** check box to add an X, so that the order of pages will be reversed.

4 Make any other settings in the Print Document dialog boxes and choose **Print** to print all odd numbered pages.

5 Put the finished, printed pages back in the paper tray, face down.

6 Click the **Reverse** check box again to remove the check mark.

7 Open the Print menu and choose **Even pages**.

8 Choose **Print** to print the remaining pages of your document on the backs of the odd numbered pages.

Duplex Printing

Reducing the Printed Image

If you are searching for a stat camera to reduce or enlarge a design you've created in PageMaker, you have missed the mark. PageMaker will reduce or enlarge anything placed on the page. Here's how:

1 Note the page number of the page containing the items you want to reduce or enlarge.

2 Choose the Print command on the File menu to open the Print Document dialog box.

3 Enter the page number for the page you want to print in the **Range** text box. Then, click the **Paper** button.

4 In the Print Paper dialog box **(Figure 19)** move to the Scale area and enter the percentage of reduction or enlargement for the page. You can enter any percentage from 5 to 1600 in as small as 1/10th percent increments.

5 Click **Print** to print the reduction or enlargement.

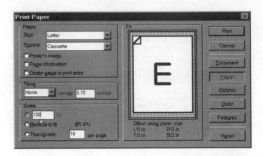

Figure 19 *Enter the amount of reduction in the Scale text box, in the Print Paper dialog box.*

Reducing and Enlarging

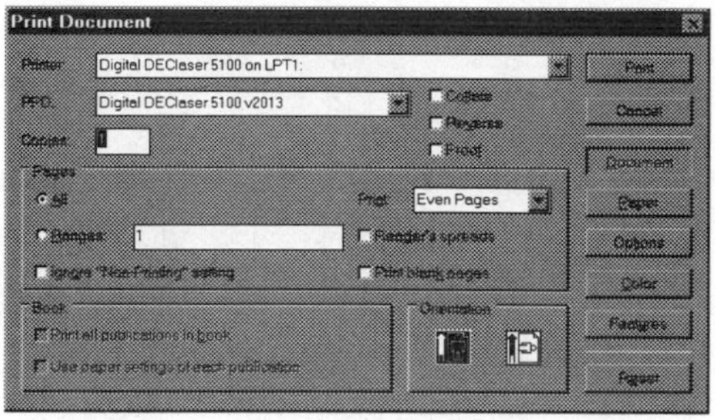

Figure 20 *Print Document dialog box.*

Figure 21 *Print oversize images by tiling pages with the Print Paper dialog box.*

Printing Larger than the Paper

Just because your laser printer takes paper no larger than letter size is no size limitation on PageMaker. I know a design firm that uses PageMaker to produce gigantic banners for store fronts. Here's how:

1 Choose the Print command on the File menu to open the Print Document dialog box **(Figure 20)**.

2 Click the **Paper** button to open the Print Paper dialog box **(Figure 21)**.

3 In the **Tiling** area, click open the Tiling menu and select **Auto**. Auto tiling lets PageMaker divide up the document page into tiles the size of the paper that runs through the printer. Once printed, all the tiles fit back together to create the larger size page.

4 In the Overlap area, enter the amount of overlap for each tile. The default setting is a ¾–inch overlap.

5 Click **Print** to begin printing the tiles.

Tiling

Adding Crop Marks

Crop marks, or trim marks, show where the edge of the document is, and where to align it in a paper cutting machine. In order to see crop marks, the size of the paper must be larger than the page size of the document. If not, then you must reduce the document to fit on the page. Here's how to add crop marks to your documents:

1 Choose the Print command on the File menu to open the Print Document dialog box.

2 Click the **Paper** button to see the Print Paper dialog box **(Figure 22)**.

3 Look in the Paper area of the dialog box and click the **Printer's marks** check box to add an X. Printer's marks include crop marks, registration bullets, color bars and density bars **(Figure 23)**.

4 Choose the **Print** button to print your document.

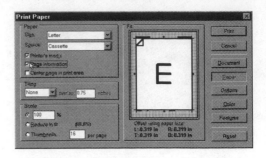

Figure 22 *Print Paper dialog box sets crop marks and registration bullets on your pages.*

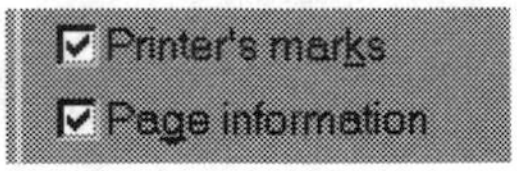

Figure 23 *Click both check boxes to add crop marks, registration bullets, and notations about color plates to your document pages.*

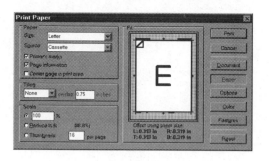

Figure 24 *Print Paper dialog box.*

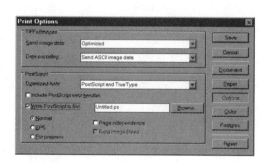

Figure 25 *Print Options dialog box sets up your document for printing to a PostScript file.*

Creating PostScript Files for a Service Bureau

Unless you are a proud owner of a 1200 dpi laser printer—as I am—you will probably want a prepress service bureau to run the final output of your pages on a high resolution imagesetter. Even I use a service bureau when I need more sharpness than my laser printer can provide, or when I need film output. PageMaker can create PostScript files which any service bureau can download to their imagesetter. Here's how:

1 Choose the Print command on the File menu to open the Print Document dialog box.

2 Click **Paper** to open the Print Paper dialog box **(Figure 24)** and choose the size paper the service bureau's imagesetter will use. Then, choose the **Printer's marks** and **Page information** check boxes.

3 Click the **Options** button to open the Print Options dialog box **(Figure 25)**. Click the **Write PostScript to file** check box. If you are not separating colors, click the **Normal** radio button. If you have separations, click the **For prepress** radio button. PageMaker will create a file name for the PostScript file in the text box (click **Save as** to change the name or location where the file will be created). See Chapter 12 for the steps to creating color separations.

4 Notice that the Print command button has changed to the Save button. Click **Save** to create and save the PostScript file.

Quick and Easy Work Habits

▪ Before sending the job off to the service bureau, give your commercial printer a quick call and ask these questions:

▪ Do you want film or paper? If film, do you want right reading or wrong reading film? Do you want film positives or film negatives?

▪ PageMaker normally prints right-reading (emulsion-side up) film. To print film wrong reading, in which the emulsion side of the film is down, choose the **Mirror** check box in the Print Color dialog box. How can you tell which side of the film the emulsion is on? Hold the film up to the light and look along the edge. One side will be very shiny, the other side will be both shiny and dull. The side with the dull areas is the emulsion side of the film.

▪ Generally speaking you will usually want film positives to give to your commercial printer. If negative film is required, click the **Negative** check box in the Print color dialog box.

▪ Before creating PostScript files for a service bureau, give them a call and discuss the job. Ask the paper size to choose, the orientation of the paper, the size of the job and the turnaround time.

Quick Work Tips

Separating Color Pages

Introduction

IN ORDER FOR A commercial printer to print more than one color on paper, the second—and any additional colors—must be separated from the principal color, which is normally black. That separation used to be done manually by creating an overlay, aligned to the black-printing art (called the *base art*) for each color used on the page. If you had black type with a red border, the border would be removed from the base art and added to an overlay, aligned to the base art with registration bullets. When your commercial printer got the work, each overlay would be photographed as a negative and a color plate made of each negative. In the above example there would be two plates, black and red: the black plate printed all the base art, the red plate printed the red border.

Now, PageMaker creates the separations for us, in much the same way artists used to do by hand. PageMaker divides the objects on the page by separate color and produces an overlay, or *color sep,* for each color used on the page. Printed on paper by a 300 dpi laser printer, the separations can be accurately proofed. Printed on film by a 1200 dpi (or higher) PostScript imagesetter, the separations can be sent directly to your commercial printer who can produce color printing plates directly from the film. The result is a significant savings to you, and often more accurate printing for your job.

Knocking Out Colors

When it is necessary to print one color over another color, you may want to remove the underlying color so its tint does not change the tint of the overprinting color. For example, if the underlying color is dark and the overprinting color is light, the darker color will show through the lighter color and change its tint. Creating a knock out (or *knocking out* the color) removes the underlying color **(Figure 1)**. As long as the overprint color is considerably darker than the underlying color, a knockout is not necessary. PageMaker knocks out underlying colors automatically, unless you are adding black text as the overprinting color.

Figure 1 *Left illustration has knocked out background so darker colors doesn't alter lighter color of character. In right illustration, the character overprints the lighter background.*

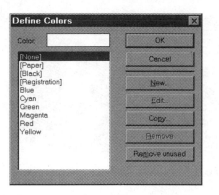

Figure 2 *Define Colors dialog box.*

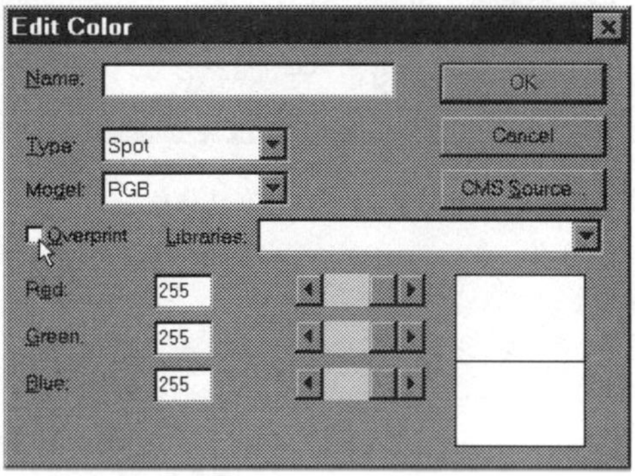

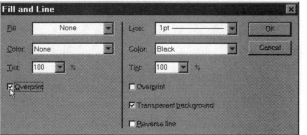

Figure 3 *Edit Color dialog box determines which colors overprint.*

Overprinting Colors

To prevent PageMaker from automatically knocking out colors, you must choose an overprint option when defining colors, or when adding lines and fills to the page. To overprint a particular color:

1 Choose the Define Colors command on the Element menu to open the Define Colors dialog box **(Figure 2)**.

2 Select the color you want to overprint and click **Edit** to display the Edit Color dialog box **(Figure 3)**.

3 Click the **Overprint** check box to add an X. Then hold down the Control key and click OK to return to your document.

To overprint lines or fills:

4 Click the line or fill you want to overprint.

5 Choose the Fill and Line command on the Element menu to open the Fill and Line dialog box **(Figure 4)**.

6 Click the **Overprint** check box to add an X for the fill and/or the line.

Tip

■ A quick shortcut to reach the Edit Color dialog box for a particular color is to open the Colors palette, and hold down the Control key while you click the color you want to edit. PageMaker will immediately display the Edit Color dialog box for the color you selected.

Figure 4 *Overprinting of lines and fills is controlled by the Fill and Line dialog box.*

Overprinting

Separating Spot Colors

Instead of being blended from varying proportions of the process colors cyan, magenta, yellow and black, spot colors are pre-mixed by your commercial printer, in much the same way special colors of house paint is mixed. Then the specially mixed ink is printed on the page. Each spot color that you define and use in your document must have its own separation in order to be printed by your commercial printer.

To separate spot colors:

1   Define the spot colors you want for your document and add them to your pages.

2   Open the Print Document dialog box **(Figure 5)** and choose the **Paper** button.

3   In the Print Paper dialog box **(Figure 6)**, click the **Printer's marks** and **Page information** check boxes to add crop marks, registration bullets and color sep labels to each separation.

4   Click the **Color** button to open the Print Color dialog box **(Figure 7)**. Click the **Separations** radio button. Then, move through the list of inks using the scroll bar. For each of your spot colors, plus Black and any process colors used in your document, highlight the ink and click the **Print this ink** check box to add a check mark beside the ink.

5   Click **Print** to print your color seps.

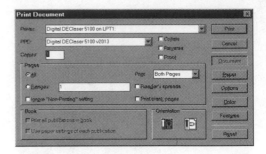

Figure 5 *Print Document dialog box.*

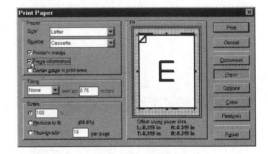

Figure 6 *Print Paper dialog box.*

Click Separations

Click each of the Spot colors

And click the Print this ink box to add a check mark

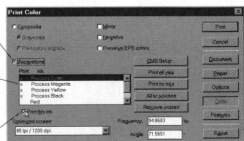

Figure 7 *Print Color dialog box*

Separating Spot Color

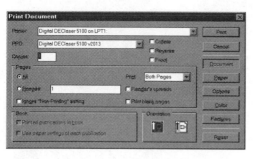

Figure 8 *Print Document dialog box.*

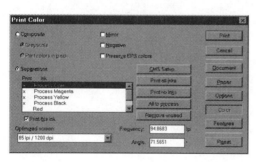

Figure 9 *Print Color dialog box.*

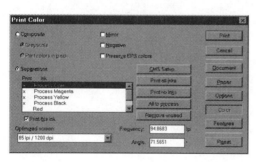

Figure 10 *Choose each process color and click the Print this ink check box to add a check mark beside the colors.*

Separating Process Colors

Process separations are produced similarly to spot separations in PageMaker. The chief difference is that since all process colors are some blend of cyan, magenta, yellow, and black, you are separating only four colors, instead of a number of different spot colors. A typical brochure, which may have any number of single colors, plus the flesh tones of color photographs, can be created with process separations alone.

1 Open the Print Document dialog box **(Figure 8)**, and choose the **Paper** button.

2 In the Print Paper dialog box, click the **Printer's marks** and **Page information** check boxes to add crop marks, registration bullets and color sep labels to each separation.

3 Then click the **Color** button to open the Print Color dialog box **(Figure 9)**. For each of the process colors, cyan, magenta, yellow and black click the ink to select it and click the **Print this ink** check box to add a check beside the ink **(Figure 10)**.

4 If your printer allows a choice of screen resolutions, choose the resolution you want in the Optimized screen menu.

5 Click **Print** to print the separations.

Tip

■ If you are proofing separations on a laser printer, and your paper size is 8½ by 11 inches, you will have to reduce the size of the page in the Print paper dialog box in order to see crop marks and color separation labels. Choose the **Reduce to fit** button, and PageMaker will automatically reduce the page size enough to include the information outside the trim area.

Quick and Easy Work Habits

◾ When you add a number of spot colors to a lengthy document, remember to check to see that the colors are assigned consistently across all the pages. The easiest way to verify spot colors is to print separations of each spot color individually. Then, if say, column rules are supposed to be in Pantone 425, and you print the spot separations for that Pantone color, it will be obvious when a colored object, such as the rule, is missing. Here's how to print individual spot colors:

1 Simply open the Print dialog box and move to the Print Color dialog box.

2 Then scroll down the list of inks and choose the first spot color. Click the **Print this ink** check box to add a check mark beside the ink, and Choose Print to print the separation.

3 Repeat for each spot color listed in the Ink menu.

◾ If you are using a high resolution imagesetter to produce separations for your commercial printer, it is better to run the separations on film rather than resin-coated paper. Any dot screens on the paper separations will have to be replaced by your printer before negatives are shot and plates can be made—the interim negative step destroys the crispness of the dot pattern. However, by providing film output, you eliminate the negative step, and your commercial printer can go directly to plates.

Quick Work Tips

Tables of Contents

13

PAGEMAKER USES AN EXTREMELY simple, yet slightly confusing means of collecting table of contents entries. It relies on you checking a check box in the Paragraph Specification dialog box **(Figure 1)** in order to tell PageMaker that a particular paragraph should be copied as a table of contents entry. Ordinarily, you might think that means paragraphs full of text, and how could they become entries in a TOC? And you'd be right in your thinking. Just remember the definition of a paragraph in PageMaker: any text ending in a paragraph return code (¶) is a paragraph. Therefore, chapter titles are paragraphs, major and minor headings are paragraphs, all of which can become the basis for your table of contents if you designate each one of them by checking the **Include in table of contents** check box.

Click here to mark headings
for a table of contents

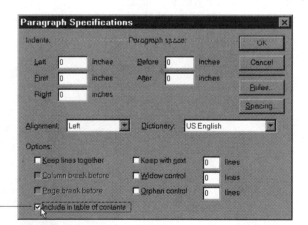

Figure 1 *Paragraph Specifications dialog box is the key to marking heading and subheadings for a table of contents.*

Figure 2 *Styles palette.*

Hooking Styles to a TOC

Instead of manually paging through your document marking each heading and sub-heading as a table of contents entry, use a heading style to automatically mark the headings and subheadings for you. Here's how:

1 Open the Window menu and choose the Styles command to display the Styles palette **(Figure 2)**.

2 Choose the Headline style in the palette, hold down the Control key and click the style name. You will see the Edit Style dialog box **(Figure 3)**.

3 Click the **Para** button to open the Paragraph Specifications dialog box **(Figure 4)**.

4 Now click the **Include in table of contents** check box to add an X.

5 To save the change, hold down the Option key and Click OK to move directly back to the Styles palette.

Now, whenever you assign a heading with the Headline style, you will automatically mark the heading to be included in a table of contents.

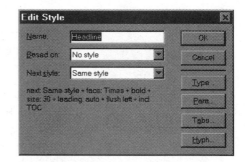

Figure 3 *Edit Style dialog box.*

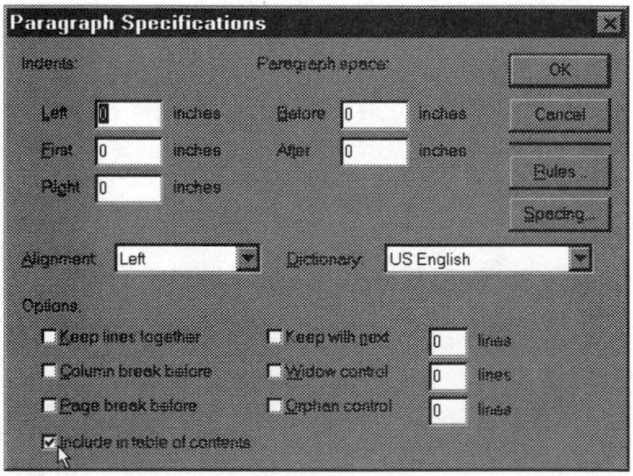

Figure 4 *Paragraph Specifications dialog box tags headings for the TOC.*

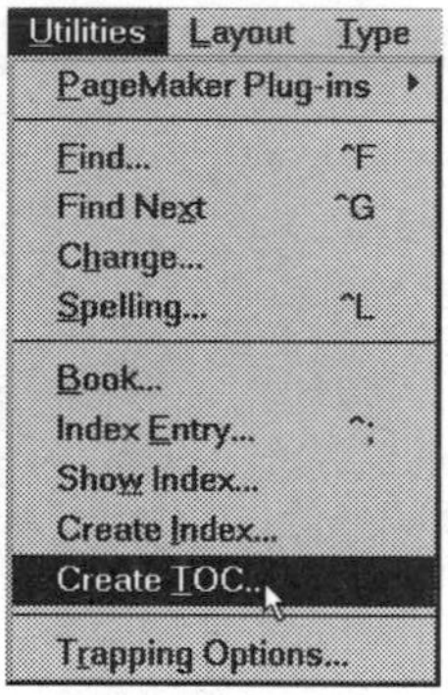

Figure 5 *Choose the Create TOC command on the Utilities menu.*

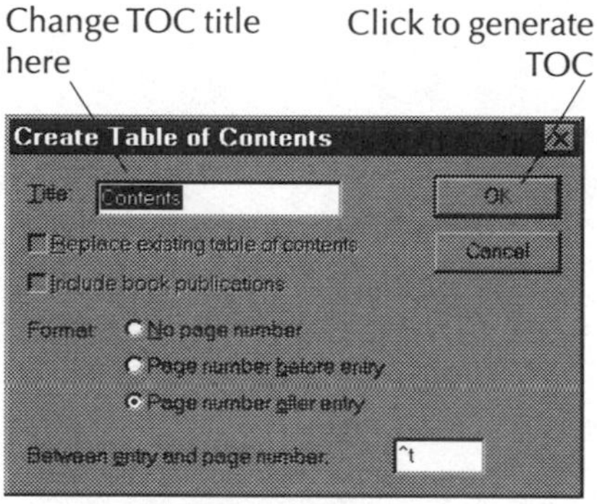

Change TOC title here   Click to generate TOC

Figure 6 *Create Table of Contents dialog box.*

Formatting and Generating the TOC

Once you have marked all heading and subheadings as table of contents entries (or used styles to do the entry marking for you), the next step is to format the TOC.

1 Move to the first page of your document, or move to the page you have designated to hold the table of contents.

2 Click open the Utilities menu and choose the Create TOC command **(Figure 5)**.

3 PageMaker will display the Create Table of Contents dialog box **(Figure 6)**.

4 Use this simple dialog box to decide how you want the page numbers situated in relationship to the TOC entries.

5 Click **Replace** existing table of contents if you have already generated a TOC and you want to revise it.

6 Enter a title for your table of contents.

7 Click OK to generate the TOC. PageMaker will assemble all the headings you have marked for inclusion in a TOC, put them in order, note their respective page numbers, and create the table of contents.

Generating the TOC

Creating Other Front Matter Tables

Once the table of contents is generated, it becomes a text block on the page, just like any other text block. If you want to create other front matter lists, such as lists of illustrations, lists of figures, or lists of tables, you can easily do so after having created the TOC. Here's how to create a list of figures (the same steps apply to any front matter list you want to generate):

1 Choose the Define styles command on the Type menu to open the Define Styles dialog box.

2 Click the **New** button to open the Edit Styles dialog box **(Figure 7)**. Create a new style called Figure Captions.

3 Format the style as you want it, but be sure to click the **Para** button to open the Paragraph Specifications dialog box. Click the **Include in table of contents** check box to add an X.

4 Save the style and assign it to all figure captions in your document.

5 Now, choose the Create TOC command on the Utilities menu. In the Create Table of Contents dialog box, enter the name **List of Figures** as the title.

6 Now, click OK to generate the list. PageMaker will gather all the figure captions, add them to the list of figures at the front of your document, and show their respective page numbers. You can follow the same steps for any kind of list.

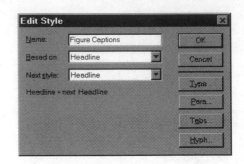

Figure 7 *Use the Edit Style dialog box to tag any type of heading, caption or title to create a front matter list.*

Other Front Matter Lists

Building an Index

A GOOD INDEX CAN make the difference between a mediocre publication and a really useful publication. The index is used as much if not more than the table of contents as a reference tool to find information. The usefulness of an index is determined by the skill and cleverness with which it is built. Luckily, in the indexing department, PageMaker makes it relatively easy to create powerful indexes.

If there is a key to creating a useful index, it is to put yourself in the place of the new reader, and try and guess what key words, subjects and topics the reader will probably search for. As an example, while readers of this book might search the index for the topic "Indexing," to learn how to create an index, they might also look under "Key words," or "Cross references," or "Finding information." All may mean the same to a beginning desktop publisher, so all those topics should be included in the index for this book. If I were writing a highly specialized book targeted to expert designers, the index could contain much more specialized jargon, because it would be a fair assumption that more knowledgeable readers would understand more technical terms.

Introduction

Adding an Index Entry

1 Open the story you want to index in the story editor by clicking the insertion point in the story and pressing **Ctrl+E**.

2 Use the text tool to highlight the word you want to add to your index.

3 Open the Utilities menu and choose the Index Entry command **(Figure 1)**.

4 PageMaker will open the Add Index Entry dialog box **(Figure 2)**.

5 Enter the primary, secondary and tertiary topics in the topic text boxes. Press Tab to move among the text boxes.

6 To see one of the topics you've already entered in the index, click **Topic**.

7 Click **Add** to add the topic, plus its secondary and tertiary topics (if any) to the index.

8 You can continue adding topics if you want, just remember to click **Add** to add each topic to the index before leaving the dialog box.

Tips

■ The fast shortcut to the Add Index Entry dialog box is **Ctrl+;**.

■ To see any existing index entry, highlight the index marker with the text tool and press **Ctrl+;**.

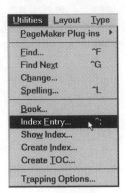

Figure 1 *Choose the Index Entry command on the Utilities menu.*

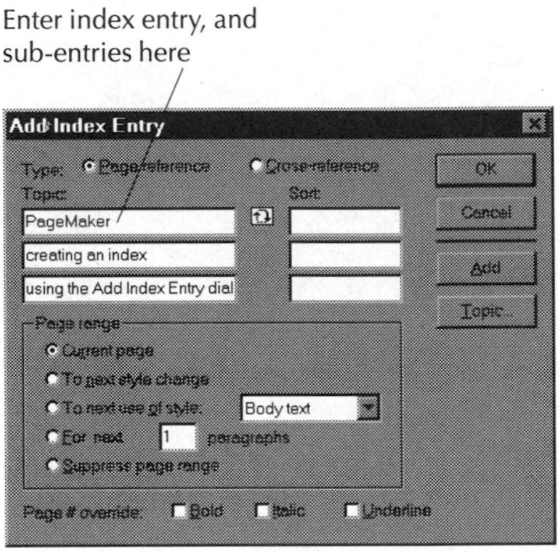

Enter index entry, and sub-entries here

Figure 2 *Enter index keywords in the Add Index Entry dialog box.*

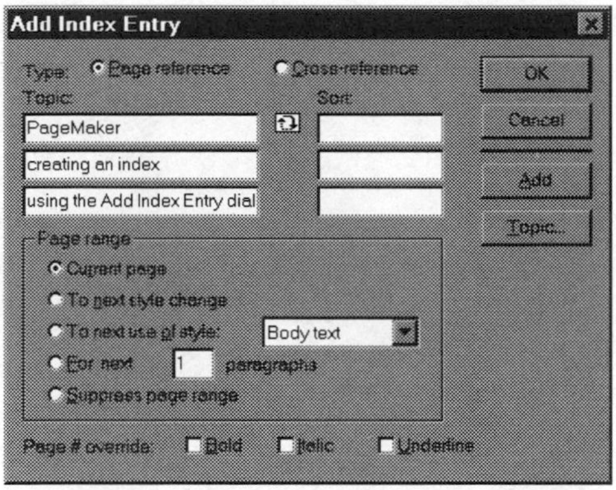

Add Index Entry

Type: ⦿ Page reference ○ Cross-reference

Topic: Sort:
PageMaker

creating an index

using the Add Index Entry dial

Page range
⦿ Current page
○ To next style change
○ To next use of style: Body text
○ For next 1 paragraphs
○ Suppress page range

Page # override: ☐ Bold ☐ Italic ☐ Underline

OK · Cancel · Add · Topic...

Figure 3 *Add Index Entry dialog box.*

Select Topic

Level 1:
Level 2:
Level 3:

Topic section B ▼ Next section

OK · Cancel · Add · Import

Level 1	Level 2	Level 3
Blocks	used in running rigg...	

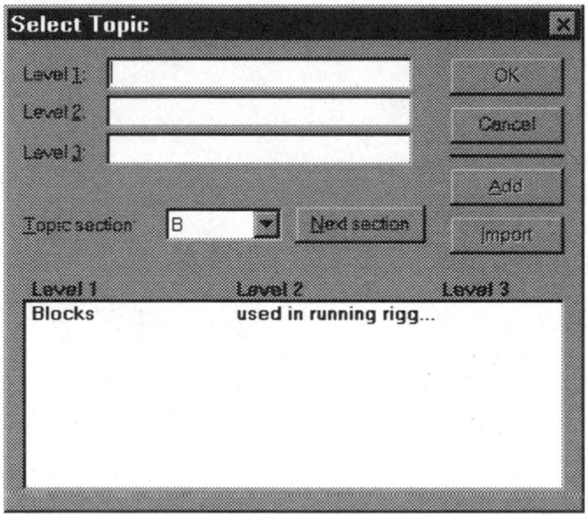

Figure 4 *Select Topic dialog box.*

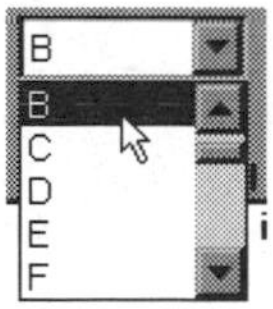

Figure 5 *Click open the topic selection menu and choose the area you want to see.*

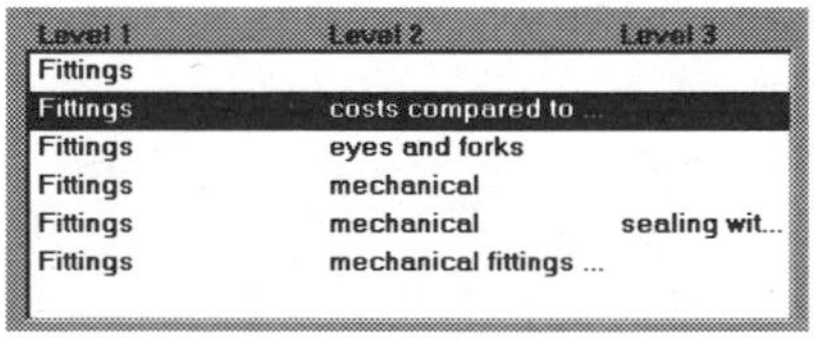

Level 1	Level 2	Level 3
Fittings		
Fittings	costs compared to ...	
Fittings	eyes and forks	
Fittings	mechanical	
Fittings	mechanical	sealing wit...
Fittings	mechanical fittings ...	

Figure 6 *Choose the level 1,2, and 3 entries you want to add to the Entry dialog box.*

Choosing Topics and Subtopics

The topics button in the Add Index Entry dialog box shows you all past entries. To keep the index consistent, refer to the topics if you are adding another entry on a subject already indexed to keep the entry wording the same. For example, unless your memory is very good, you might add several index entries that are slightly different—like *rigging, wire rigging* and maybe *rigging wire*—all which you really want under the same topic called "Rigging." By using the Topic button, you can avoid having to edit the slightly different entries later on.

1 Once in the story editor, open the Add Index Entry dialog box **(Figure 3)** by pressing **Ctrl+;**.

2 Before typing a new entry, check to see if you have already entered a similar entry by clicking the **Topic** button.

3 PageMaker will open the Select Topic dialog box **(Figure 4).** Open the Topic section menu **(Figure 5)** and select the alphabetical sections you want to review **(Figure 6)**.

4 If you find an existing topic, click it to add to the Level 1–3 text boxes. Click OK to return to the Add Index Entry dialog box.

5 The topics and any subtopics will be added automatically to the three topic text boxes **(Figure 7)**. Make any changes you want to the wording and click OK to save the entry.

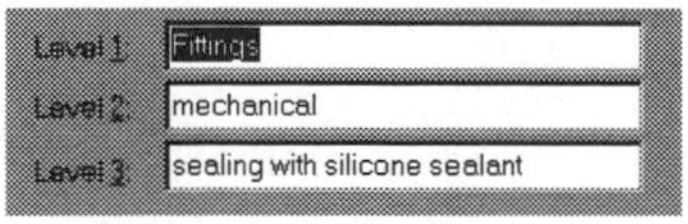

Level 1:	Fittings
Level 2:	mechanical
Level 3:	sealing with silicone sealant

Figure 7 *PageMaker adds the duplicate entries for you automatically.*

Topics and Subtopics

Controlling Index Entry Page Numbers

Once you have entered an index entry, you must tell PageMaker the kind of page number you want. The Add Index Entry dialog box defaults to recording the individual page number where the index entry marker is added. But you can choose to show a range of page numbers if the material you are indexing spans more than one page. Here's how to control page numbers:

1   Open the Add Index Entry dialog box and add an entry to the topic text boxes **(Figure 8)**.

2   To use the page where you added the index marker, leave the default Page range setting of **Current page**.

3   To include pages for text that discusses the topic until a style change is encountered, choose **To next style change**.

4   To include a range of pages to a designated style change, choose **To next use of style** and choose the style you want to designate from the style menu.

5   To include a range of pages for a certain number of paragraphs following the paragraph containing the index marker, choose **For next 1 paragraphs** and enter the number of paragraphs instead of the number 1.

6   To withhold the page range altogether, choose **Suppress page range**.

7   Choose OK to save the index entry and page range you set up.

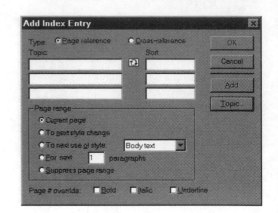

Figure 8 *Add Index Entry dialog box.*

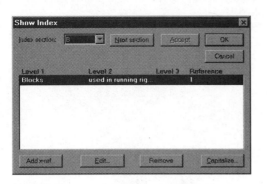

Figure 9 *Show Index dialog box.*

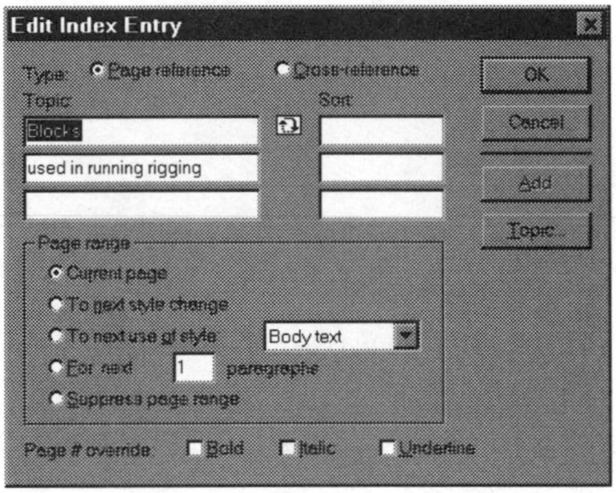

Figure 10 *Correct inconsistencies and misspellings using the Edit Index Entry dialog box.*

Reviewing Accumulated Topics

It's a good idea to take a look at the index entries you are accumulating. It keeps the topics fresh in your mind, and, I think it helps head off mistakes.

1 Open the Utilities menu and choose the Show Index command. PageMaker will open the Show Index dialog box **(Figure 9)**.

2 The dialog box collects and assembles in alphabetical order all the index entries you have made. If you have linked chapters of a book together using the book command, you will see the entries to the current document plus all other documents that comprise the "book."

3 This dialog box is similar to the Select Topic dialog box we looked at earlier in that you can move alphabetically to any topic. Yet, here you see what the actual index entries will look like.

4 You can correct any misspellings by choosing the **Edit** button and editing the entry in the Edit Index Entry dialog box **(Figure 10)**. Click OK to save the changes and return to the Show Index dialog box.

5 Add a cross reference to any entry by choosing the entry and clicking the **Add X-ref** button.

Reviewing the Index

About Cross References

Instead of duplicating index entries, a cross reference basically sends the reader from one topic in an index to another topic. PageMaker designates a cross reference by adding *See* before the entry. Sometimes you may want to send the reader to collateral entries—terms similar to the index entry. PageMaker defines this type of collateral cross-references with *See also* in front of the term. **Figure 11** shows two types of cross references.

This cross reference sends the reader to another entry ————

This entry offers pages for references but suggests additional reading under another topic ————

Norseman. *See* Fittings: mechanical

Rigging. *See also* Standing rigging
Adding mechanical terminals 5
replacing swagged fittings 1
running rigging 1
shrouds and stays defined 2
standing rigging 1

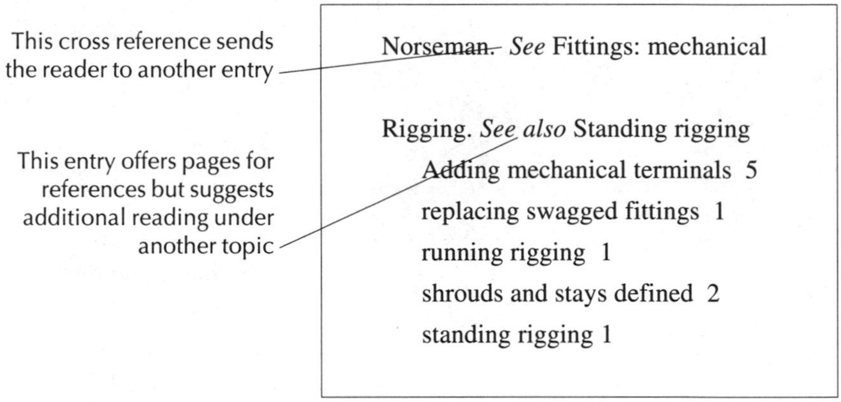

Figure 11 *Two different types of cross references in a PageMaker index.*

Cross Referencing

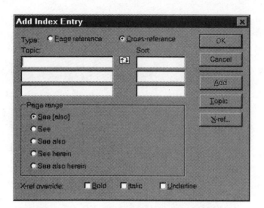

Figure 12 *Cross reference part of the Add Index Entry dialog box.*

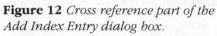

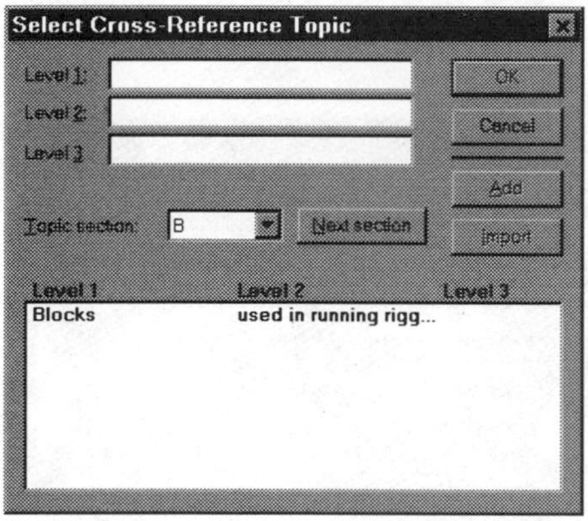

Figure 13 *Select Cross–Reference Topic dialog box.*

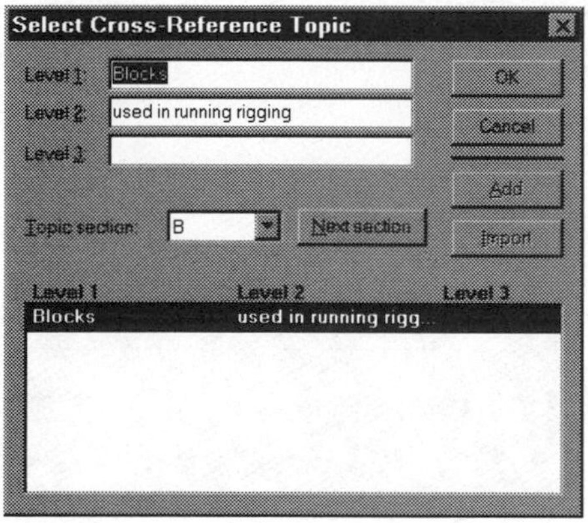

Figure 14 *Clicking the topic in the list adds it to the topic boxes.*

Adding Cross References

1 Open the Add Index Entry dialog box by pressing **Ctrl+;**.

2 Click the **Cross-reference** radio button **(Figure 12)**. Note that a cross reference consists of two parts, the from-topic (the initial index entry that you find in the index) and the to-topic (where the cross reference sends you).

3 Enter the from-topic in the three topic text boxes.

4 If you want a page number reference for the from-topic click the **See [also]** button. If you don't want a page number reference for the from-topic, click the **See** radio button.

5 Now, to create the to-topic, click the **X-ref** button to open the Select Cross–Reference Topic dialog box **(Figure 13)**. If you know the exact to-topic, type it in the Level 1 text box (and add any secondary or tertiary subtopics in the Level 2 and level 3 boxes).

6 If you are unsure of the exact wording for the to-topic, click the **Topic section** button and move to the alphabetical category for the topic. Double click the to-topic you want to add it to the Level 1,2, and 3 boxes **(Figure 14)**.

7 Click OK to move back to the Add Index Entry dialog box, and click OK again to go back to your document.

Tip

- While PageMaker stores cross references much the same way as index topics, it does not add an index marker. So, to find, and correct or change a cross reference, you must use the Show Index dialog box. Find the cross reference and choose **Edit** to change or modify it.

Cross Referencing

Reviewing Accumulated References

1 Open the Utilities menu and choose the Show Index command. PageMaker will open the Show Index dialog box **(Figure 15)**.

2 The dialog box collects and assembles in alphabetical order all the index entries and cross references you have made. If you have linked chapters of a book together using the book command, you will see the entries to the current document plus all other documents that comprise the "book."

3 Find the cross references by looking in the last column to the right for the reference **See also...** or **See...** You can correct any misspellings by choosing the **Edit** button and editing the entry in the Edit Index Entry dialog box **(Figure 16)**. Click OK to save the changes and return to the Show Index dialog box.

Tip

■ To automatically capitalize words in topics and subtopics, click the Capitalize button to open the Capitalize dialog box **(Figure 17)**.

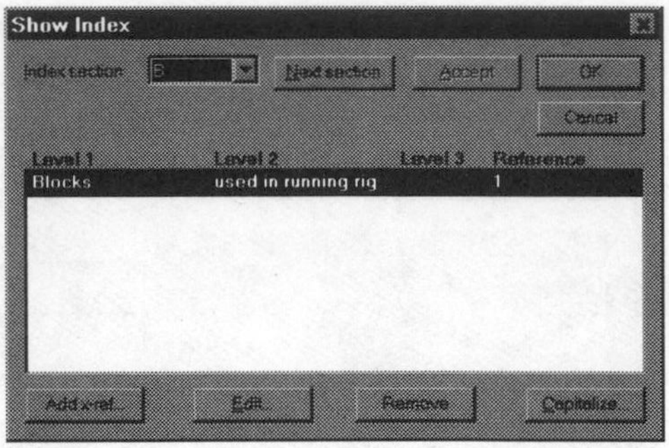

Figure 15 *Show Index dialog box lets you see all the entries you've added.*

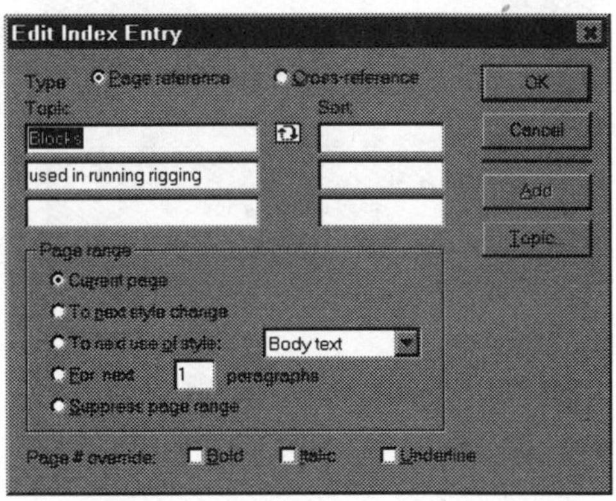

Figure 16 *Modify your cross references with the Edit Index Entry dialog box.*

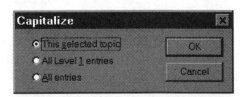

Figure 17 *Automatically capitalize entries with the Capitalize dialog box.*

Cross Referencing

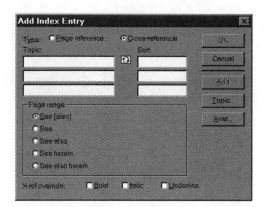

Figure 18 *Use the X-ref override check boxes to modify the style of cross reference entries.*

Changing the Cross Reference Type Styles

To make the cross references stand out a little more in your index you can make some rudimentary type style changes.

1 Open the Add Index Entry dialog box by pressing **Ctrl+;** and click the **Cross-reference** button **(Figure 18)**.

2 Notice the X-ref override area. Click the **Bold** check box to bold the to-topic. Click **Italic** to italicize the to-topic. Click **Underline** to underline the to-topic. **Figure 19** shows examples of the overrides.

Norseman. *See* **Fittings: mechanical**

Rigging. *See also* **Standing rigging**
    Adding mechanical terminals 5
    replacing swagged fittings 1
    running rigging 1
    shrouds and stays defined 2
    standing rigging 1

Norseman. *See Fittings: mechanical*

Rigging. *See also Standing rigging*
    Adding mechanical terminals 5
    replacing swagged fittings 1
    running rigging 1
    shrouds and stays defined 2
    standing rigging 1

Norseman. *See* <u>Fittings: mechanical</u>

Rigging. *See also* <u>Standing rigging</u>
    Adding mechanical terminals 5
    replacing swagged fittings 1
    running rigging 1
    shrouds and stays defined 2
    standing rigging 1

Figure 19 *Cross–reference overrides in Bold, Italic and Underline shown.*

Cross Referencing

Generating the Index

Once all entries have been added, all cross references added, and entries and cross references checked for consistency of wording, it's time to take a crack at generating the index.

1 Move to the page where you want to position the index.

2 Choose the Create Index command on the Utilities menu to open the Create Index dialog box **(Figure 20)**.

3 Change the Index title if you wish.

4 If this is a revision to an existing index, you probably want to check the **Replace existing index** check box (if this is the first attempt at creating the index, the option will be grayed out).

5 Click OK. PageMaker will generate the index and display a loaded text icon. Position the icon and click the mouse to place the index text.

Tip

▪ If your index takes more than a page or two, turn on Autoflow (on the Layout menu) so PageMaker will create as many additional pages as it needs to automatically place the index for you.

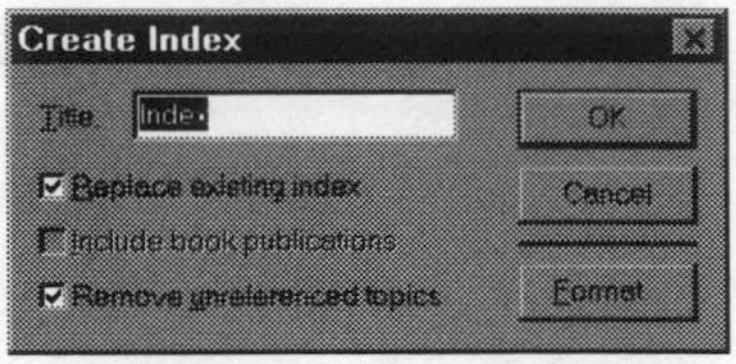

Figure 20 *Create Index dialog box.*

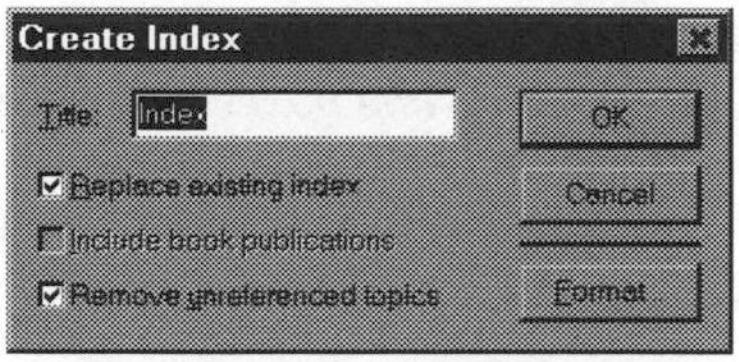

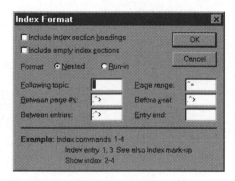

Figure 21 *Create Index dialog box.*

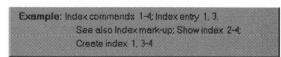

Figure 22 *Change the index format with the Index Format dialog box.*

Changing the Index Format

The default index format works very well for most situations. Look at the index for this *Visual QuickStart Guide*, which was created with PageMaker. It's considered a nested format, where each level of sub-topic, under a main topic, is indented, or nested, so as to show its subordination. To change the format:

1 Choose the Create Index command on the Utilities menu to open the Create Index dialog box **(Figure 21)**.

2 Click the **Format** button to open the index Format dialog box **(Figure 22)**.

3 To delete the alphabetical letter sections in the index, click **Include index section headings** to *remove* the X. PageMaker will create the index with extra space to designate a section change but without section letters.

4 To change the nested format to a run-in type format, click the Run-in button. An example of the different format is shown in the example area **(Figure 23)**.

Example: Index commands 1-4; Index entry 1, 3.
See also Index mark-up; Show index 2-4;
Create index 1, 3-4

Figure 23 *Example of run-in format as opposed to nested index entries.*

Quick and Easy Work Tips

■ A quick shortcut for creating an index entry is **Ctrl+;**. To mark a word or phrase in text as an index entry, highlight the word with the text tool and press **Ctrl+;**.

■ Regardless of the temptation, it's best to add index entries while working in the story editor. Here you can get comfortable, see the index symbols, and know exactly where you are adding a new entry. Remember, to move to the story editor, click the text tool anywhere in the text block you want to index and press **Ctrl+E**.

■ Once you have added index entries to a document—which really should be the very last step before final printing—be extremely careful when editing text, especially deleting text. If you must edit, do so in the story editor, where you can see the index entry markers. An editor once deleted 90 percent of the index entries I had added to a book laid out in PageMaker by editing in the layout view and blindly deleting my index markers.

■ You should develop a system for locating the index markers. I generally place them immediately to the left of key words in text. If I'm indexing a broader topic, I will usually add them to the subhead introducing the broad topic. Entries are easier to locate and change if you formulate a means of positioning them.

■ The easiest way to double-check your index prior to generating it is to use the Show Index command on the Utilities menu. In the Show Index dialog box scroll through each alphabetical section and look for misspellings, and multiple entries that are slightly different; for example the entries *dialog box, dialog boxes, dialogue boxes* and *dialogue box*

should be cleaned up to be just one entry, probably *dialog boxes*. To make each multiple entry the same, click the **Edit** button, make your corrections, and click OK.

Checking Spelling

PAGEMAKER'S SPELLER OFFERS YOU editing control after text is imported into text blocks. Although the speller lacks some of the sophisticated options of spelling programs in word processors, it can handle the job of checking spelling, and finding some kinds of errors, like internal capitalization and duplicate words.

The speller works by comparing each word of text with its list of more than 100,000 words. Whenever exceptions are found, the speller stops and waits for your help in deciding how to handle the exception. It may be that the word is spelled correctly, but it is not in PageMaker's dictionary. The exception may be caused by an alternative spelling such as the word *acknowledgement* and *acknowledgment*. The former is a recognized alternative spelling, yet, PageMaker will stop on the word and suggest the latter as the correct spelling.

Introduction

Starting the Speller

The speller is accessible only from the story editor.

1 Click the text tool insertion point any-where in the text block you wish to spell-check and press **Ctrl+E** to open the story editor.

2 Choose the Utilities menu and click Spelling to display the Spelling dialog box **(Figure 1)**.

3 To begin spell-checking the text block containing the insertion point, click **Start**. To check all stories in your docu-ment (all independent text blocks), click the **All stories** radio button.

4 Unlike most other dialog boxes in PageMaker, to close the Spelling dialog box you must click the Close box.

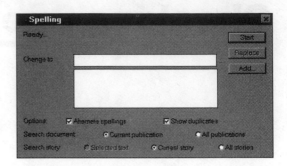

Figure 1 *Spelling dialog box.*

Choosing Spelling Options

1 From the story editor, open the Utilities menu and choose the Spelling command to display the Spelling dialog box **(Figure 2)**.

2 Click the **Alternate spellings** check box if you want PageMaker to suggest alternate spellings in the list of possible words.

3 Choose **Show duplicates** if you want PageMaker to stop on duplicate words.

4 You can ask the speller to search words in only the current publication, or all opened publications—click the appropriate radio button.

5 The search stories options refer to checking independent text blocks in your document. To spell check all text blocks, choose **All stories**.

Figure 2 *Set options the way you want in the Spelling dialog box.*

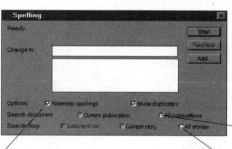

Click to spell all opened documents

Click to have the speller suggest words

Click to spell all text block in your document

Setting Spelling Options

Correcting Misspelled Words

Now that the speller is open and you've selected the options you want, let's start:

1 Click **Start** to begin spelling.

2 When the speller encounters a word it doesn't know, it stops and displays the word **(Figure 3)**. Notice that the word in question is displayed twice: marked as an improper word and shown in the Change to text box. If you click **Alternate spellings**, you will also see PageMaker's version of the word **(Figure 4)**.

3 If the spelling is correct (and PageMaker just doesn't know it) click **Ignore** and the speller will continue. If the Spelling is correct and you want to add the alternate spelling to PageMaker's dictionary, click **Add**.

4 If the spelling is indeed wrong, you can either click the insertion point in the Change to text box and correct the word yourself. Or, you can click the correct spelling from the list of suggestions. In either event, click the **Replace** button to correct the word.

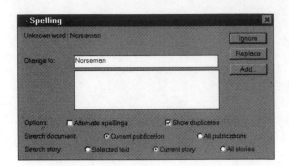

Figure 3 *Spelling dialog box displays a word it doesn't know.*

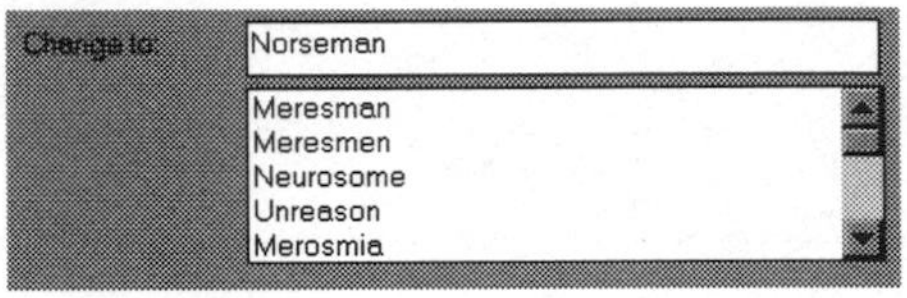

Figure 4 *The Alternative Spellings option lets PageMaker offer some suggestions.*

Correcting Words

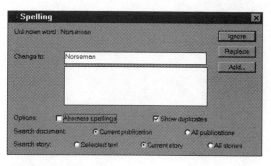

Figure 5 *Spelling dialog box with unknown word.*

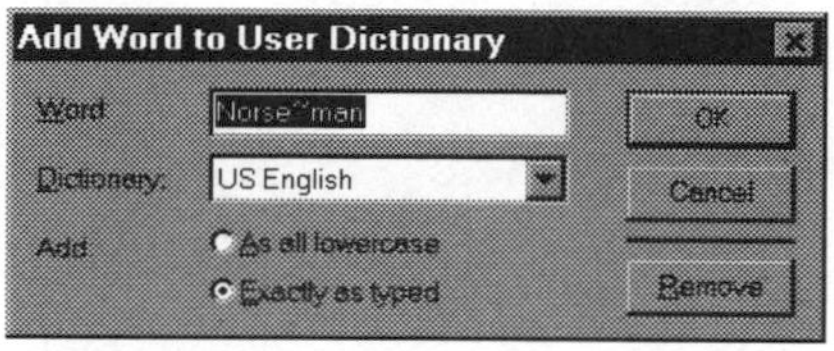

Figure 6 *Add to User Dictionary dialog box lets you add words to the spelling and hyphenation dictionary.*

Adding Words to the Dictionary

PageMaker comes with a very replete dictionary which it uses for spell checking and hyphenation. To add or delete words:

1 Open the Spelling dialog box **(Figure 5)** and click the **Add** button to open the Add to user dictionary dialog box **(Figure 6)**.

2 If the speller stopped on a word in question, the word will be shown, with PageMaker's attempt at dividing it into syllables, in the Word text box. If the word is broken correctly, click OK to add the word.

3 If the syllable breaks for the word are wrong, click in the text box and make the correction. Tildes (~) indicate where PageMaker can hyphenate the word. One tilde shows PageMaker the most advantageous place to hyphenate the word; two tildes indicate the next most advantageous and three tildes indicate the least desirable place to break the word.

4 To remove a word, type it in the Word text box (you needn't add the syllable breaks) and click **Remove**.

Tips

■ If you go through the steps to remove a word that isn't in the dictionary, PageMaker will ignore the request and display a notice saying the word in question can't be found.

■ You don't have to add a word to the dictionary just to spell it correctly. If you know you'll be using a word in text, and want PageMaker to hyphenate it correctly, add the word to the dictionary, taking care to break the word as you want it. PageMaker will be able to hyphenate it as well as check its spelling.

Adding Words to the Dictionary

Quick and Easy Work Habits

▪ Spelling should be the very last thing you do before printing. When the Spelling dialog box is opened, be sure to click the **All stories** button, which checks every word on your pages, including headers and footers, even callouts like those used in the figures of this book.

▪ If you are working on text in the story editor, you can open the Spelling dialog box and drag it down to the very bottom of the screen, so that only its title bar shows. Then it's instantly available for you to move between the story editor and the speller.

▪ Remember to not place too much trust in the speller. It does a fine job of comparing your words with those of its dictionary. However, it has no idea what you are trying to say, so it will not catch mistyped words, such as *its* for *it's*, *is* for *his*, *there* for *their*, or *bought* for *ought*.

Quick Work Tips

Using Find and Change

16

PAGEMAKER'S FIND AND CHANGE commands let you substitute one word or phrase with another, or one set of criteria for type and paragraphs with another. You can, for example, search for all occurrences of *Windows* and substitute *Windows 95*. Search for *PageMaker version 5.0* and substitute *PageMaker version 6.0*. Look for all instances of the phrase *Aldus PageMaker* and replace them with *Adobe PageMaker*.

But the two commands can handle a lot more than just word substitution. The real power of Find and Change is the ability to search for one font and substitute another, or find all instances of a font size or style, and replace them with a different size and style. Find and Change can also look for styles and replace them with different styles. All very powerful features that can save you enormous time in editing your documents.

One word of caution. PageMaker will take you literally if you tell it to look for one thing and replace it with another. It doesn't care how that action might screw up your document. So be careful using the commands, double check to make sure of what you are about to replace, and by all means save your document before performing a find and replace. That way if something is messed up, you can simply revert to the saved version before you activated the Find and Change commands.

Chapter 16

Finding Words

While the Find and Change commands go hand-and-hand, you can use just the Find command to locate specific words or phrases in your document. Here's how:

1 In the story editor, open the Utilities menu and choose the Find command **(Figure 1)**. PageMaker will display the Find dialog box **(Figure 2)**.

2 Enter the word or phrase you want to search for in the **Find what** text box. Take care in typing the word or phrase exactly as it appears in text.

3 To match the case (uppercase or lower-case) of the word or phrase in text, choose the **Match case** check box. Note if the word or phrase is used in both upper and lower case, selecting Match Case will mean that PageMaker will match only the case of whatever you have typed in the dialog box.

4 Choose the **Whole word** check box to keep PageMaker from finding the search word as a part of a larger word; for example, searching for *figure* and finding *configure*.

5 Now click **Find** to begin the search. After PageMaker finds the first occurrence, the Find button changes to the **Find next** button.

Tip

▨ If you are unsure of the exact spelling of a word, use a wildcard character to change one or more letters in the word. The characters ^? tell PageMaker to consider any character. For example, if you want to find *exegesis* but you're not sure if it is spelled exegesis or exigesis, you might enter ex^?gesis as the search word. The wildcard character means PageMaker will find the word regardless of the third letter.

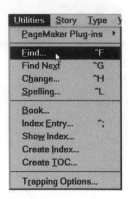

Figure 1 *Choose the Find command on the Utilities menu.*

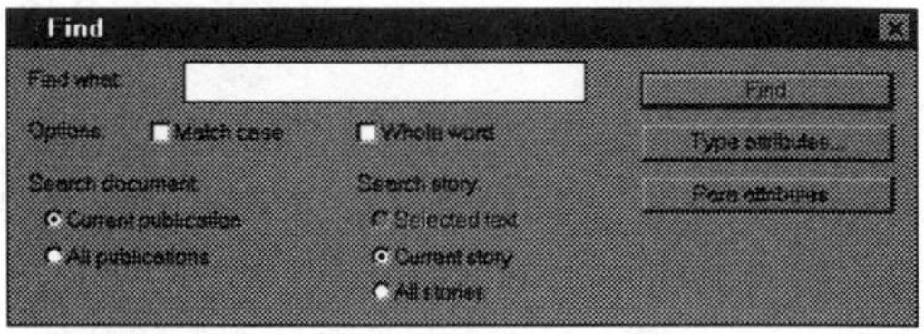

Figure 2 *Find dialog box.*

Find Words

Figure 3 *Find dialog box can not only find words but attributes of type.*

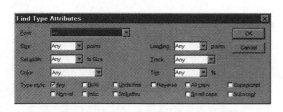

Figure 4 *Find Type Attributes dialog box searches for different type specifications.*

Finding Type Attributes

Let's say you've used a font in your document that now you want to change. If you tied all text in your document to styles, you could simply change the styles. However, if some text is floating around without a style, use the Find command to locate it.

1 Choose the Find command on the Utilities menu to open the Find dialog box **(Figure 3)**.

2 Leave the Find what text box empty. Choose the **Type attributes** button to open the Find Type Attributes dialog box **(Figure 4)**.

3 Click open the **Font** menu and select the font you want to search for.

4 You can also select any other type attribute, such as type size, color, style, etc.

5 Click OK to return to the Find dialog box.

6 Now, click the **Find** button to begin the search. PageMaker will look through your document, and stop at the first occurrence of the font you selected.

Tip

■ The find command begins its search at the insertion point position and searches forward to the end of your document. If the insertion point wasn't at the beginning of the document, when the Find command reaches the end, it will display a dialog box asking you if you want it to wrap the search back to the start of the document and search the text before the insertion point.

Finding Type Attributes

187

Finding Paragraph Attributes

PageMaker searches for paragraph attributes in much the same way as type attributes.

Figure 5 *Find dialog box can also search for paragraph attributes.*

1 Open the Find dialog box **(Figure 5)**, and leave the Find what text box empty. Choose the **Para attributes** button to open the Find Paragraph Attributes dialog box **(Figure 6)**.

2 Click open the **Para style** menu and select any of the style you have defined for you document.

3 Or, search for a particular paragraph alignment by clicking the **Alignment** menu.

4 Finally, you can search for paragraphs where leading is based on a particular method of measurement. Click OK to return to the Find dialog box.

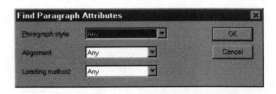

Figure 6 *Find Paragraph Attributes dialog box looks for several different paragraph specifications.*

5 Now, click the **Find** button to begin the search. PageMaker will look through your document, and stop at the first occurrence of the paragraph attribute you selected.

Tip

▎ Here's how to easily find force-justified paragraph lines. You remember forced-justified lines, don't you? They are usually the last lines of justified paragraphs that are a bit shy of being justified to the right margin. Aligning just the ending line as force-justified means the line is stretched to the right margin. Well, to find the forced lines and make sure they look acceptable, use the Find command. Click open the **Para attributes** button and open the Alignment menu. Then choose **Force justify**. Click OK to return to the Find dialog box and click the **Find** button to locate the first incident of using force justify in your document.

Finding Paragraph Attributes

Figure 7 *Change dialog box searches and replaces words and phrases.*

Replacing Words

The Change command is the action side to the Find command. When you choose it, you see the same basic Find dialog box with additional boxes and buttons to not only find something but replace it with something else.

1 Choose the Change command on the Utilities menu to open the Change dialog box **(Figure 7)**.

2 Enter the word or phrase you want to search for in the Find what list box.

3 Enter the word or phrase you want to substitute in the Change to text box.

4 Click **Find** to locate the first instance of the word or phrase you're searching for. Then click **Change** to change it to what you want.

5 To find the next occurrence click **Find next**, or click **Change & find** to automatically find the next occurrence and change it.

6 Click **Change all** to find and change all occurrences of the word or phrase.

Tip

■ A quick shortcut to the Change dialog box is press **Ctrl+H**.

Finding and Changing Type Attributes

1 Press **Ctrl+H** to open the Change dialog box (**Figure 8**).

2 Click **Type attributes** to open the Change Type Attributes dialog box (**Figure 9**).

3 In the Find area, enter the **Font** you want to search for. Choose any other attributes you want to change.

4 In the Change to area, select the replacement font and any other attributes you want to include. The dialog box might look like **Figure 10**. Click OK to return to the Change dialog box.

5 Now, click **Find** to locate the first occurrence of the attributes you selected in the Find area. When PageMaker encounters them, click **Change** to covert the attributes to what you selected in the Change to area.

Figure 8 *Use the Change dialog box to search and replace type attributes.*

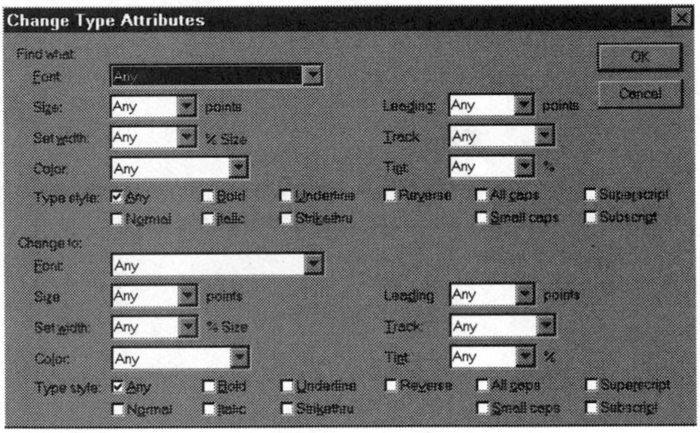

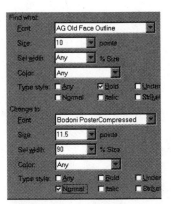

Figure 9 *Choose the attributes you want to find and what you want to replace them with in the Change Type Attributes dialog box.*

Figure 10 *Change Type Attributes dialog box ready to do some finding and changing.*

Changing Type Attributes

Figure 11 *Choose Para attributes to search and replace paragraph attributes.*

Finding and Changing Paragraph Attributes

1 Press **Ctrl+H** to open the Change dialog box **(Figure 11)**.

2 Click **Para attributes** to open the Change Paragraph Attributes dialog box **(Figure 12)**.

3 In the Find area, enter the paragraph style, alignment or leading method you want to search for.

4 In the Change to area, select the replacement attributes you want to include. The dialog box might look like **Figure 13**. Click OK to return to the Change dialog box.

5 Now, click **Find** to locate the first occurrence of the attributes you selected in the Find area. When PageMaker encounters them, click **Change** to convert the attributes to what you selected in the Change to area.

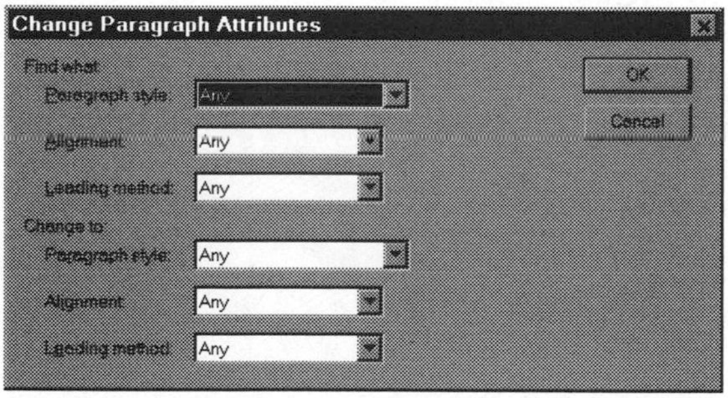

Figure 12 *Look for paragraph attributes and change them to other attributes.*

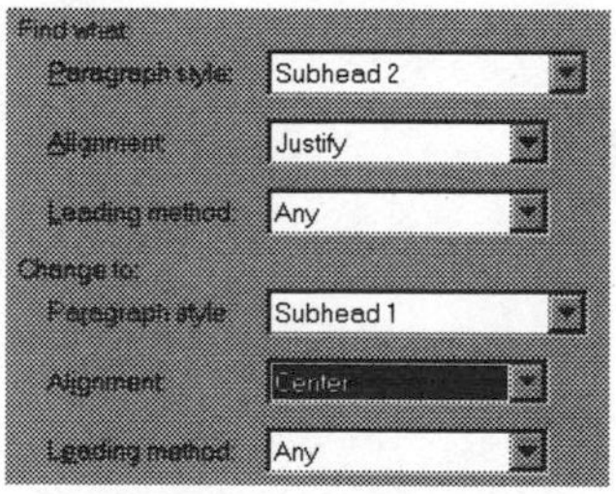

Figure 13 *Change Paragraph Attributes ready to go with a search and replace.*

Finding and Changing Special Characters

PageMaker uses a number of special codes to control certain printing and non-printing characters. For example, each time you press the Return key, you add a non-printing code to the end of the text line, called a *hard return code*. PageMaker represents a hard return code with the special code ^p. You can run Find and Change on many of PageMaker's special characters. The table below lists the more useful characters.

To find or change this	Type this in the Change dialog box
em dash	^_ (underline character)
em space	^m
en dash	^=
en space	^>
hard return	^p
index entry marker	^;
inline graphic marker	^g
page number marker	^# or ^3
tab	^t
thin space (.25 em)	^<

Understanding Plug-Ins

PLUG-INS ARE WHAT ALDUS called *additions* in version 5.0 of PageMaker. Basically plug-ins are external programs that add special capabilities to PageMaker. You use plug-ins just as you would any other command on a menu in PageMaker. All plug-ins are located on the Utilities menu by choosing the PageMaker Plug-ins command. We won't cover all the plug-ins tha come with PageMaker, but we will look at some ways of saving you time in creating your documents by using some of the more useful plug-ins.

Introduction

Add Continuation Line Plug-in

This command adds continuation lines to the top or bottom of your pages. Continuation lines say something like "Continued on page 15" at the bottom of a page, and "Continued from page 14" at the top of the page.

1. Click the text block you want to add a continuation line to with the Pointer tool.
2. Choose Add Cont'd Line from the list of plug-ins to open the Continuation notice dialog box **(Figure 1)**.
3. Choose whether the notice should go at the top or bottom of the page.
4. Click OK to create the continuation line **(Figure 2)**.
5. Finally, move to the continued page, and create the corresponding continuation line there following steps 1–4.

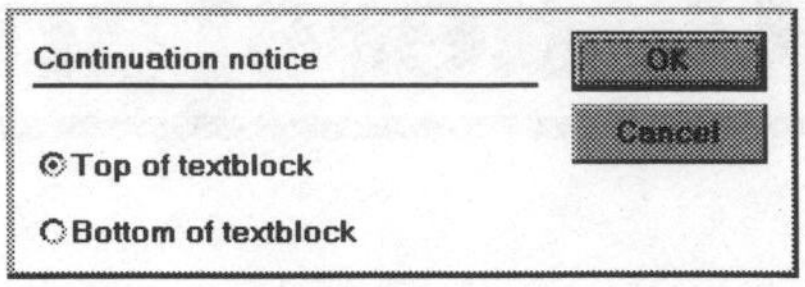
Continuation notice
OK
Cancel
Top of textblock
Bottom of textblock

Figure 1 *Continuation notice dialog box.*

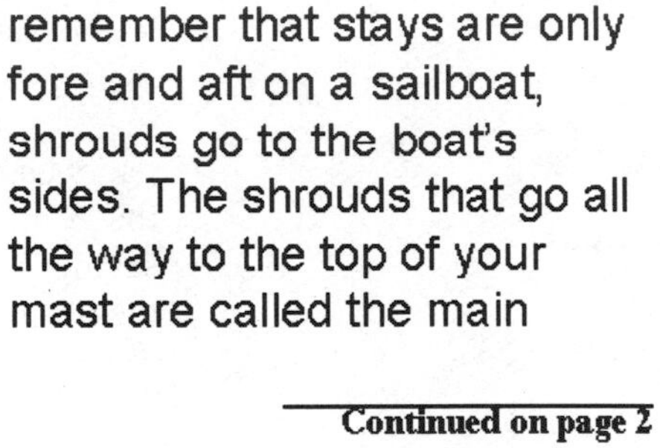
remember that stays are only fore and aft on a sailboat, shrouds go to the boat's sides. The shrouds that go all the way to the top of your mast are called the main
Continued on page 2

Figure 2 *Example of continuation notice added to bottom of text block.*

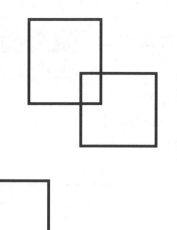

Figure 3 *To align object start with two or more objects and select them.*

Align Objects Plug-in

This plug-in lets you align several selected items in relationship to themselves and to different alignment schemes.

1 Begin by selecting the items you want to align by Shift–clicking with the Pointer tool **(Figure 3)**.

2 Choose Align Objects from the plug-in list to open the Align Objects dialog box **(Figure 4)**.

3 Click the alignment button that best shows how you want the object arranged. For this example let's choose a vertical center line scheme **(Figure 5)**.

4 Since this is a vertical arrangement, move to the Vertical area and set a distribution distance. Let's say .5 inch.

5 Now, click OK to align the objects. In a moment the objects will rearrange themselves like **Figure 6**.

Figure 4 *Choose an alignment scheme in the Align Objects dialog box.*

Figure 5 *Click the alignment button that best depicts how you want the objects aligned.*

Figure 6 *Click OK and the plug-in aligns the objects according to what you specified.*

Align Objects

195

Balance Columns Plug-in

This plug-in balances multiple columns to either the top or bottom of the page.

1 Select between two and 40 columns by Shift–clicking with the Pointer tool.

2 Choose the Balance columns plug-in from the menu to open the Balance columns dialog box **(Figure 7)**.

3 Choose how you want to align the columns: from the top or from the bottom, and click the appropriate button.

4 Then, decide where leftover lines should be added: to the bottom of the first column or the bottom of the second, and click the appropriate button.

5 Click OK to align the columns based on your selections in the dialog box.

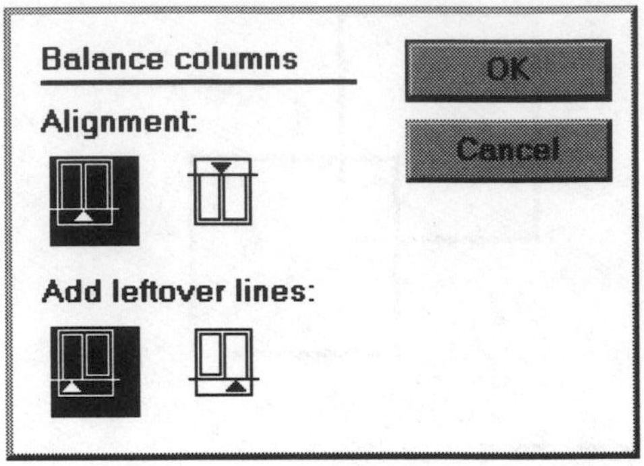

Figure 7 *Balance columns dialog box.*

Balance Columns

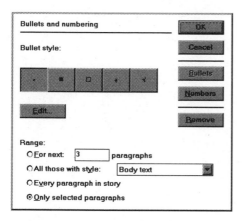

Figure 8 *Bullets and numbering dialog box.*

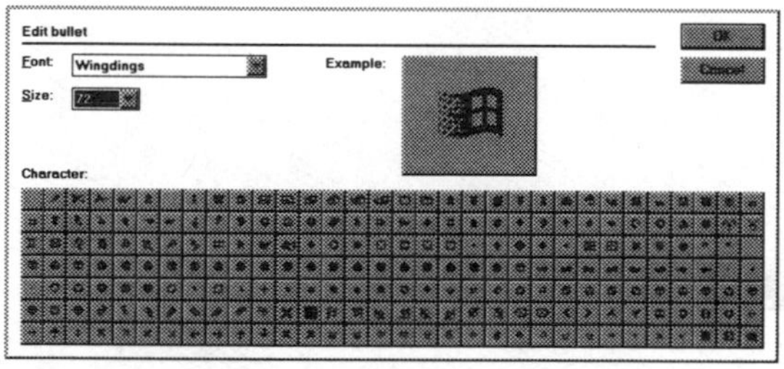

Figure 9 *Choose a different bullet in the Edit bullet dialog box.*

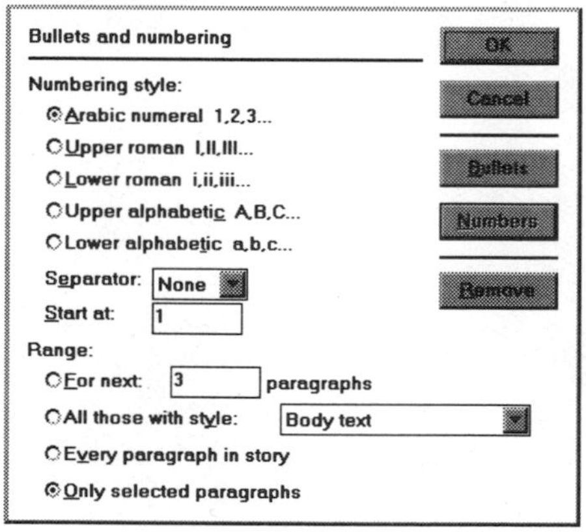

Figure 10 *Numbers view of the Bullets and numbering dialog box.*

Bullets and Numbering Plug-in

Here is a simple way of creating bulleted or numbered lists in your documents. The plug-in configures the bullets or numbers for you and adds them to the number of paragraphs you specify.

1 Click the Text tool insertion point anywhere in the first of several paragraphs you want bulleted or numbered.

2 Choose the Bullets and numbering command on the Plug-in submenu to open the dialog box **(Figure 8)**.

3 To specify a bullet style, click the bullet you want from the list, or click **Edit** to select a different bullet. You will see the Edit bullet dialog box **(Figure 9)**. Choose a new bullet symbol and a size and click OK to return to the Bullets and numbering dialog box.

4 In the Range area, select how many consecutive paragraphs the bullets or numbers should be applied to.

5 To add numbers to your paragraphs, click the **Numbers** button, and choose the style of number you want **(Figure 10)**.

6 Finally, click OK to add the bullets or numbers to your paragraphs.

Bullets and Numbering

Drop Cap Plug-in

A drop cap is a large initial letter that begins a paragraph and drops down a number of lines into the paragraph. This plug-in makes adding drop caps to paragraphs quick and easy.

1   Click the Text tool in the paragraph you wish to add a drop cap to.

2   Choose the Drop cap command on the Plug-in submenu to open the Drop cap dialog box **(Figure 11)**.

3   In the Drop cap area, enter the number of lines you want the letter to drop into. Click **Apply** to see the results of your setting.

4   To apply another drop cap to either the previous or next paragraph in the text block, click **Prev** or **Next** respectively.

5   Click OK to save the drop caps you have prepared and return to your document.

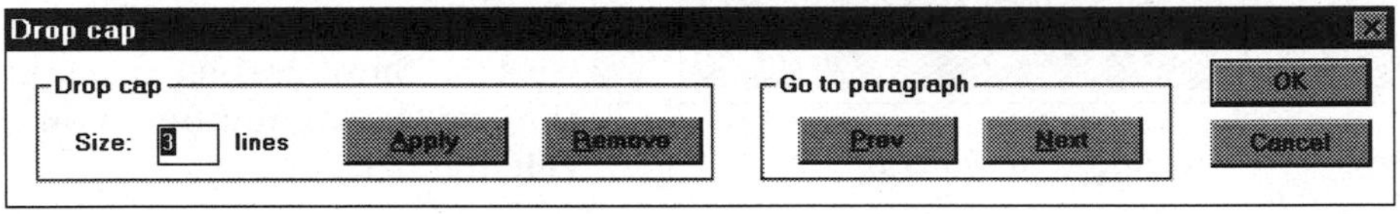

Figure 11 *Drop cap dialog box.*

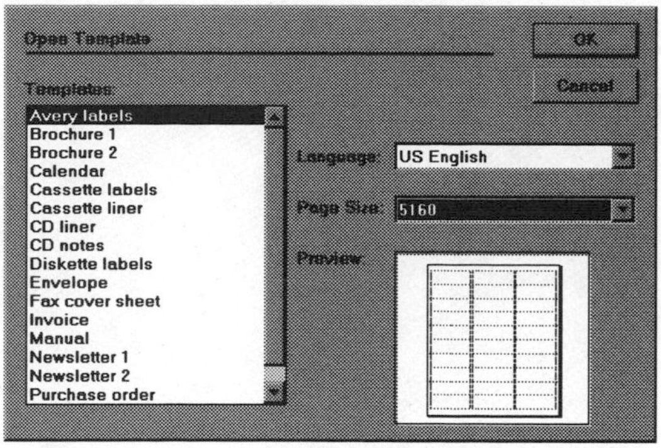

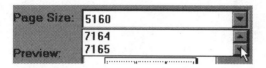

Figure 12 *Open Template dialog box.*

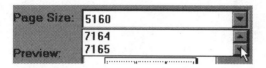

Figure 13 *Paper size menu for Avery labels template.*

Open Template Plug-in

PageMaker comes with a number of templates, ready for you to use as is or modify with your own ideas. You open and use templates with the Open template plug-in.

1 Choose the Open Template command on the Plug-in submenu to display the Open Template dialog box **(Figure 12)**.

2 Scroll down the list of templates and choose the one you want to open.

3 For most of the templates, you have the choice of different paper sizes. Click open the Paper size menu to see your choices. In the case of the Avery labels, the menu lets you choose which Avery label you want to use, based on the Avery numbering system **(Figure 13)**.

4 Click OK to open the template as a new, unnamed document.

Open Templates

Sort Pages Plug-in

This plug-in allows you to move and rearrange the sequence of pages in your document.

1 Choose the Sort pages command on the Plug-in submenu to open the Sort pages dialog box **(Figure 14)**.

2 To move a page from one position to another, click the page you want to move, say page 61, and drag it between the page you want it to be and the next sequential page. If you want page 61 to really be page 63, then click and drag page 61 between pages 63 and 64 **(Figure 15)**. Release the mouse button and the order will be changed **(Figure 16)**.

3 Note that the new order of pages, plus the original order is shown below the page icons.

4 When you are through sorting pages, click OK to perform the sort and return to your document.

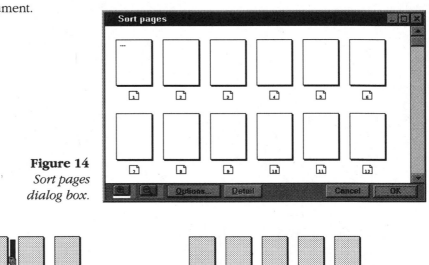

Figure 14
*Sort pages
dialog box.*

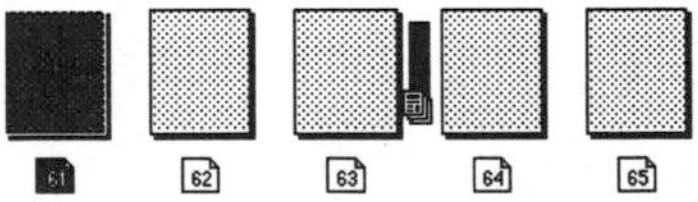

Figure 15 *Drag a page between two other pages to move the page of your document.*

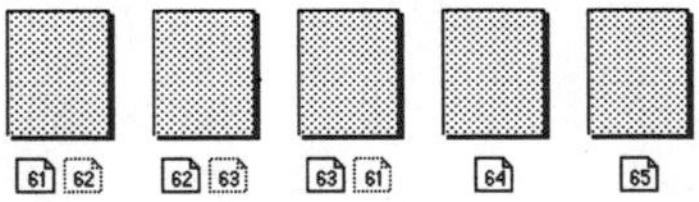

Figure 16 *The rearranged pages show their old and new page numbers.*

Creating Books

ONE OF PAGEMAKER'S POWERFUL features is the ability to invisibly link individual documents together into a book. Whether you are creating a book like this one, or some other long document, such as a magazine, proposal, sales presentation, technical publication, or journal—regardless of what you call it—if it contains separate sections, chapters or parts that will eventually be bound together in some way, PageMaker's Book command can save you enormous time and energy.

The Book command asks you to create a list, in order, of the individual documents that will make up your publication. For this *Visual QuickStart Guide*, for example, I listed the front matter, the table of contents, each of the chapters, the two appendices and the index, in order. Then PageMaker combined them together, and renumbered all the pages in consecutive order. It also linked together all the individual headings in order so that I could create a master table of contents for all documents. And, it combined all the marked index entries, so one master index would include all the documents in the book list.

This chapter explains how PageMaker's Book command works, and the steps you must take to create a "book" containing individual PageMaker documents.

Introduction

Combining Chapters Using the Book Command

1 Open any document that will be included in the book list.

2 Click open the Utilities menu and choose the Book command **(Figure 1)**.

3 You will see the Book Publication List dialog box **(Figure 2)**.

4 The book list on the right contains the individual PageMaker documents you want to link together into a book. Use the list on the left to locate the documents you want to add to the book list.

5 For each document that you locate, click to select it and choose the **Insert** button to add it to the list.

6 Use the **Move up** and **Move down** buttons to adjust the order of the documents in the book list. When everything is in order it will look like **Figure 3**.

7 Click OK to return to your document.

Adding Chapters to the Book

Figure 1 *Choose the Book command on the Utilities menu.*

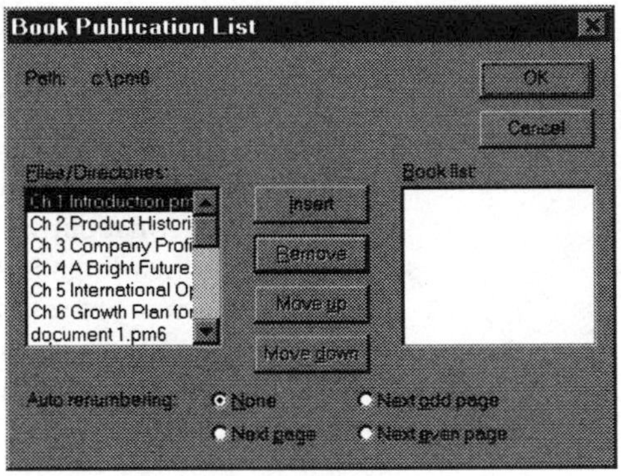

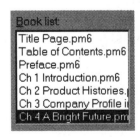

Figure 2 *Book Publication List dialog box links chapter documents together into a "book."*

Book list:

Title Page.pm6
Table of Contents.pm6
Preface.pm6
Ch 1 Introduction.pm6
Ch 2 Product Histories.
Ch 3 Company Profile i
Ch 4 A Bright Future.pm

Figure 3 *Book list with PageMaker documents in proper order.*

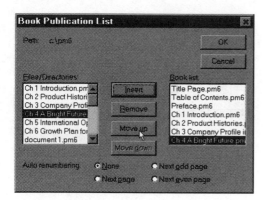

Figure 4 *Use the Move up and Move down buttons to rearrange documents in the Book Publication List dialog box.*

Rearranging the Order of Documents in the Book List

1 Choose the Book command on the Utilities menu to open the Book Publication List dialog box **(Figure 4)**.

2 To move an existing document in the Book list toward the front of the order, click the document to be moved and click **Move up**. Each time you click the button the document will take the place of the document in front of it.

3 To move an existing document in the Book list toward the back of the order, click the document and choose **Move down**. Each time you click the Move down button, the document will take the place of the document after it in the stacking order.

4 When you are satisfied with the arrangement of documents, click OK.

Rearranging Book List Order

Adding and Deleting Documents to the Book List

1 Choose the Book command on the Utilities menu to open the Book Publication List dialog box **(Figure 5)**.

2 To add another document to the book list, position the highlight bar in the book list directly above where you want to insert a document.

3 Then, find the document on the list box to the left and double click to add the document to the book list (**Figure 6**).

4 Click OK to save the book list and return to your document.

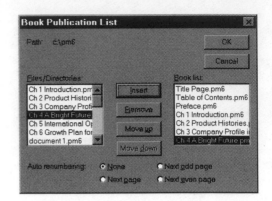

Figure 5 *Book Publication List dialog box.*

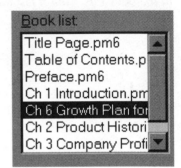

Figure 6 *Book list in Book Publication List dialog box with a document inserted.*

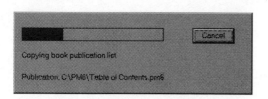

Figure 7 *PageMaker updating all documents in book list.*

Updating the Book List

Once you have the order of documents finalized, you must update all the documents in the book list with the linked information.

1 Open any other document that is a part of the book list. Notice that its document name is the only name in the book list. Add the other documents to the list in the correct order and choose OK to return to your document.

2 Hold down the Control key and choose the Book command on the Utilities menu.

3 PageMaker will display a small dialog box **(Figure 7)** that tells you it is updating the publications list. Actually, it is adding the book list to all the documents that are a part of the list.

Updating the Book List

Changing and Updating Page Numbers

The final step in preparing your book is to decide how you want to handle the consecutive number of pages.

1   Choose the Book command on the Utilities menu to open the Book Publication List dialog box.

2   Look in the Auto renumbering area. PageMaker gives you four choices to handle sequentially numbering the pages of your book:

■ **None**—Select this option if you don't want sequential numbering; each chapter will begin with page 1.

■ **Next page**—Numbers the pages of the chapters sequentially, beginning with page 1 (or a different page number if you specified in the Document Setup dialog box).

■ **Next odd page**—Traditionally, books begin chapters on right-hand pages, which normally are odd numbered pages. If you want your book to be sequentially numbered this way, choose the Next odd page option. PageMaker may have to insert blank even-numbered left-hand pages at the end of chapters to force the odd numbered pages at the beginning of chapters.

■ **Next even page**—This option is similar to the odd numbered page option except it starts each chapter on an even-numbered page. Aside from STOP proposals, popular with the aerospace industry, I don't know of any document conventions that start chapters with even numbered pages.

3   Click OK to confirm your page numbering option. PageMaker will display a message box asking if you want to update page numbers. Click **Yes** to renumber the pages of your chapters.

Keyboard Shortcuts

File Management Shortcuts

New Document	Ctrl+N
Open Document	Ctrl+O
Save Document	Ctrl+S
Save All Documents	Shift+Save
Check Links	Ctrl+=
Print Document	Ctrl+P
Quit PageMaker	Ctrl+Q

Tool Shortcuts

Pointer tool	Shift+F1
Text tool	Shift F2
Ellipse tool	Shift+F3
Rectangle tool	Shift+F4
Line tool	Shift+F5
Constrained-Line tool	Shift+F6
Polygon tool	Shift+F7
Zoom tool	Shift+F8
Rotation tool	Shift+F9
Cropping tool	Shift+F10
Magnify tool	Ctrl+Spacebar
Reducing tool	Ctrl+Shift+Spacebar

Editing and Layout Shortcuts

Copy	Ctrl+C
Cut	Ctrl+X
Paste	Ctrl+V
Power Paste	Ctrl+Shift+P
Send Object to Back	Ctrl+B
Bring Object to Front	Ctrl+F

Snap to Guides On/Off	Ctrl+Shift+5
Snap to Rulers On/Off	Ctrl+Shift+Y
Guides On/Off	Ctrl+J
Rulers On/Off	Ctrl+R
Place Text and Graphics	Ctrl+D
Insert One Page	Ctrl+Shift+"

View Change Shortcuts

Fit in Windows	Ctrl+0
50% View	Ctrl+5
Actual View	Ctrl+1
200% View	Ctrl+2
Set all pages to same view	Opt+View
Go to Page	Ctrl+/
Move to Next Page	F12
Move to Previous Page	F11

Typography Shortcuts

Increase Size 1pt	Ctrl+Shift+>
Decrease Size 1pt	Ctrl+Shift+<
Increase to Next Menu Size	Ctrl+>
Decrease to Next menu Size	Ctrl+<
All Caps On/Off	Ctrl+Shift+K
Subscript On/Off	Ctrl+\
Superscript On/Off	Ctrl+Shift+\
Kern Apart .01 em	Ctrl+Shift+R Arrow
Kern Close .01 em	Ctrl+Shift+L Arrow
Kern Apart .04 em	Ctrl+R Arrow
Kern Close .04 em	Ctrl+L Arrow

Moving Around in Text Blocks

Move to End of Line	End
Move to Start of Line	Homw
Move Up One Line	Up Arrow
Move Down One Line	Down Arrow
Move Right One Character	R Arrow
Move Left One Character	L Arrow
Move Right One Word	Ctrl+R Arrow
Move Left One Word	Ctrl+L Arrow
Down One Para	Ctrl+Down Arrow
Up One Para	Ctrl+Up Arrow
Down One Screen	Page Down
Up One Screen	Page Up

Setting Defaults by Double-Clicking Toolbox Tools

Preferences Defaults	Pointer tool
Document Setup	Alt+Pointer tool
Type Specs	Text tool
Paragraph Specs	Alt+Text tool
Fill and Line Settings	Ellipse tool
Rounded Corners	Rectangle tool
Custom Line Settings	Line tool
Polygon Settings	Polygon tool

Keyboard Shortcuts

Special Characters

Extended Characters

Bullet (•)	Ctrl+Shift+8
Copyright (©)	Ctrl+Shift+o
Trademark (™)	Alt+0153
Registered Trademark (®)	Ctrl+Shift+g
Ellipsis (…)	Alt+0133
Degree (°)	Alt+0176
Paragraph (¶)	Ctrl+Shift+7
Section (§)	Ctrl+Shift+6
Open Double Typographic Quotation Mark (")	Ctrl+Shift+[
Closed Double Typographic Quotation Mark (")	Ctrl+Shift+]
Open Single Typographic Quotation Mark (')	Ctrl+[
Closed Single Typographic Quotation Mark (')	Ctrl+]
Foot Symbol (')	Courier double quote
Inch Symbol (")	Courier single quote
English Pound (£)	Alt+0163
Japanese Yen (¥)	Alt+0165
Cent (¢)	Alt+0162

Markers

Page Number (LM)	Ctrl+Shift+3
Index Entry (◘)	Ctrl+;

Typographic Characters and Codes

Em Dash (—)	Ctrl+Shift++
En Dash (–)	Ctrl++
Em Space	Ctrl+Shift+M
En Space	Ctrl+Shift+N
Thin Space (1/4 em)	Ctrl+Shift+T
Nonbreaking Space	Opt+Spacebar
Soft Return	Shift+Return
Nonbreaking Hyphen (-)	Ctrl+Shift+-
Soft Hyphen	Ctrl+-
Nonbreaking Slash	Ctrl+Opt+/
AE Ligature (Æ)	Alt+0198
ae Ligature (æ)	Alt+0230
CE Ligature (Œ)	Alt+0140
oe Ligature (œ)	Alt+0156

Index

Index

V

W

Z

Index